REINVENTING
EVE

REINVENTING

EVE

*Modern Woman
in Search of Herself*

by Kim Chernin

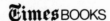

Library of Congress Cataloging-in-Publication Data
Chernin, Kim.
Reinventing Eve.
1. Women—Psychology—History.
2. Women—Mythology.
3. Women in the Bible.
4. Feminism.
I. Title.
HQ 1206.C48 1987   305.4'2   87-7106
ISBN 0-8129-1320-5

Page 191 is an extension of this copyright page.

9 8 7 6 5 4 3 2

First Edition

Book Design: Mary Cregan

To my daughter, Niki,
and her friends: Jenny, Kate, Lisa, Rachel

When God was on the point of making Eve, He said: "I will not make her from the head of man, lest she carry her head high in arrogant pride; not from the eye, lest she be wanton-eyed; not from the ear, lest she be an eavesdropper; not from the neck, lest she be insolent; not from the mouth, lest she be a tattler; not from the heart, lest she be inclined to envy; not from the hand, lest she be a meddler; not from the foot, lest she be a gadabout. I will form her from a chaste portion of the body," and to every limb and organ as He formed it, God said, "Be chaste! Be chaste!" Nevertheless, in spite of the great caution used, woman has all the faults God tried to obviate. The daughters of Zion were haughty and walked with stretched forth necks and wanton eyes; Sarah was an eavesdropper in her own tent, when the angel spoke with Abraham; Miriam was a talebearer, accusing Moses; Rachel was envious of her sister Leah; Eve put out her hand to take the forbidden fruit, and Dinah was a gadabout.

—LOUIS GINZBERG
Legends of the Bible

CONTENTS

Preface: THE WOMAN WHO IS NOT YET   xiii

Part One: INITIATION   1

Part Two: DESCENT   45

Part Three: UNDERWORLD   79

Part Four: DISOBEDIENCE   139

Notes   185

Acknowledgments   189

PREFACE:
The Woman Who Is Not Yet

I dream: I am climbing a spiral staircase. It is winding up from the underworld. I carry a heavy blanket, a folding cot, a placard, a few charred books, a handful of mud.

I reach my study; the window is open. It is a spring day; a squirrel is walking about on my papers, smearing the ink that has not dried since I lifted my pen, closed my eyes, descended into the underworld.

I sit down quietly at my desk. The squirrel scampers away, onto the windowsill. I push my papers aside and start to work with the lump of earth I have brought back. I am trying to shape a female figure. But every time I try to complete the mud-pie woman with the traditional symmetry (two breasts launched proudly upon a recognizable body), the whole thing crumbles to pieces. Finally, getting to my feet to abandon the entire project, I give it one last try. Stick a spare breast on the back of the figure. Add an extra arm to the neck. Dump one more nippled protuberance on top of the head. I stand back and look at my work. Unfinished it is, without doubt; rough-hewn and decidedly experimental, at least this figure holds together.

I become aware of a voice. It has been speaking since I left the underworld. I took it for a soft humming with something of lullaby, something of love song. Yet now, as I prop the lumpy figure upright on my desk, the voice says: "This is the New Eve. The Woman Who Is Not Yet."

I wake up fully, blinking in the light. Was it dream or vision? Did I wake or sleep? The squirrel has vanished, my papers are neatly stacked on my desk. But my hands! They are covered in mud.

The New Eve? The Woman Who Is Not Yet? I lived for a long time with these words before I understood their connection to my writing. But one day it occurred to me that for years I had been writing about the woman of the future who is struggling to emerge from us. During that time my writing project did not actually crumble to pieces. But it did undergo a curious process of proliferation. Time and again, when I sat down to describe the Woman Who Is Not Yet, I found that I had to step back from my original goal to lay the groundwork for it.

The first step produced *The Obsession*. There I discussed the way our culture's fear of female power is expressed through a sustained coercion to keep women small in size and undeveloped. Having satisfied myself that insurmountable obstacles to a woman's development arise from the culture in which she comes of age, I had to ask what it would take to bring about the further unfolding of the female psyche. It had become evident to me that women of our day were not able to get on with this brave new task our generation had inherited. The contemporary epidemic of eating disorders proved to be a generational breakdown, in which the female problem of development had moved from culture to the family, from the body to the mouth, from an obsession with weight to a preoccupation with hunger.

Consequently, in *The Hungry Self*, I took a look at the way eating disorders disguise a severe female identity crisis, which itself hides a mother-daughter struggle, both crises characteristic of this moment in which women have called into question everything that has been uttered about us since the days of Eve.

By this time I felt I could approach the question of what the new female identity might be like and how we, as women, might achieve it. If we are not to develop into pseudomen, taking on masculine attributes, clothes, and qualities, into what exactly are we to develop? My two earlier books had analyzed the obstacles. Now, at last, I might be ready to sketch a tentative map of that new development.

Meanwhile, something unexpected had arisen in these books. When I placed the individual woman's struggle for self-expression within a cultural context, it had become clear to me that our future as women would require us not merely to evolve, but to radically re-create a female psyche shaped by a culture that fears and suppresses women. Well, how else could it be? This woman we have begun to imagine will not slide smoothly into existence as a fully formed and highly polished theoretical concept. We are conceiving her out of the urgency and passion with which we live. This is no laboratory experiment we are attempting here. We are giving birth, the way women do, with mighty labor and a lot of blood, to that new being (rough-hewn, decidedly experimental, an arm sticking out of her neck, an extra breast or two wherever they might be needed), the future of our kind, perfectly unthinkable before our time, still fitfully under way.

These reflections on the Woman Who Is Not Yet are linked together by a fascination with food and by the general question why food is forbidden to modern women. Thus, the tyranny of slenderness encourages us to regard food with a sense of dread because eating leads us away from the present cultural ideal for slenderness in women and back into an older, frightening imagery of female abundance. For the hungry self food is problematic and disturbing because it reminds us of the earliest mother-daughter bond. Eve's dilemma, whether to eat or not to eat a forbidden fruit, will take us beyond present culture back to the primordial meaning of food.

What does Eve have to do with all this? In my reading of her tale Eve becomes a heroine of disobedience, our culture's first compulsive eater. Eve broke a food taboo. By eating a food she was not supposed to eat she became responsible for the fall of man. But Eve, by eating the apple, also unstitched the authority of the ruler who had established the taboo. When Eve fell, the terrifying power of the God worshipped through obedience to his diet fell with her. In this sense: Eve as rebel, the first woman to challenge the subjugation of woman in the patriarchal garden.

This reading of the Eden story is supported by an historic event. It, too, involves a food taboo, a woman who breaks it, the ending of a cultural order.

In this case, the forbidden food was a banana. The woman was the Hawaiian queen Kaahumanu, who consumed the fruit as a deliberate act of rebellion against the religious laws that subjugated women. In her time (1772–1832) women were not allowed to eat bananas, coconuts, pork, or baked dog. They could not eat with the men, or fish in salt water, or touch the nets men had laid out. A menstruating woman could not sleep in the same house as her husband. The penalty for breaking these rules was death.

Kaahumanu had been the favorite wife of King Kamehameha I. When he died she clothed herself in his feather cloak and lifted his spear. Then she persuaded his heir, Liholiho, to make her his vice-king. Outraged by the food taboos that maintained the suppression of women, Kaahumanu decided to get Liholiho to abolish them. Joining forces with Liholiho's mother, Kaahumanu set the stage for a revolt.

First, she ate the forbidden banana in the king's presence. Finally, she got the king to eat with women in the presence of the people.

"The people," writes the historian Maxine Mrantz, "though shocked, readily followed the king's example. It was as if . . . they had been waiting to destroy the kapu system. Led by the high priest, they set fire to idols. . . . Stone images were thrown into the sea. . . . Formal religion was a thing of the past in Hawaii."

This is the story of a cultural order brought down by the eating of a banana.

Eve, our rebel, has been forbidden two things in the Garden of Eden. One of them is knowledge. The other is food. She knows the risk involved but goes ahead anyway and consumes knowledge. Therefore, we ask: what kind of knowledge is this, associated with food, for which this first woman was compulsively hungering? Could it be knowledge of her capacity to become something far different than the Father God, creating her in his image, intended her to be?

For thousands of years women have had to adjust to a world created by men. Potentially capable of creating ourselves, we are not easily at home in this world where woman may only become what man wants her to be. And yet, what choice do we have? To be homeless in the only home we possess? Rootless but urgently requiring a sense of roots? If we take this world men have created as the only possible world, we cannot afford to make ourselves exiles within it. And so, we invent woman in the image of man's image of woman. High-heeled and charming, we become what we are expected to be: docile and seductive, good listeners, eager to make a good match, we long to build our nest and nourish our young and care for our man. In this form we come to know ourselves, a diminished and restricted being who pretends to be at home in the world men expound. If the Woman Who Is Not Yet is ever to exist we must discover ourselves as women apart from the woman we have invented to please men. That is where Eve and her apple enter the story.

In other mythic traditions from the ancient world the apple tree in a garden belongs to a goddess. In Avalon, "apple-land," the Celtic queen of the dead was kept busy handing out apples to Irish kings, who ate them and became immortal. Idun, goddess of apple-land in Norse mythology, fed the gods her magic apples to keep them from dying. Gaea, the earth goddess of the Greeks, brought a tree bearing golden apples to the wedding of Hera and Zeus. The tree was planted in the garden of the Hesperides and guarded by Ladon, the watchful dragon. The magic apples may not have been for just anyone, but it certainly wasn't a sin to eat them. Growing from their sacred tree, stored with the power of the Mother Goddess, they offered resurrection and immortality to those who ate them.

We begin with an eating disorder, we end with a goddess. In the oldest tales it was she who created the universe, endowed it with laws, upheld nature, presided over the birth and dying of mortals. As mother and female she was more powerful than the male gods. The supreme presence in the universe, she was sculpted in stone, called by a thousand names; she appeared in stories and myths all over the earth, was known everywhere, always the same—a deity who embodies the possibilities of female self-development.

And so we reimagine Eve, eater of the apple, as she might behave in a mythic tradition that associates tree with goddess and symbolically invites the daughter to partake of the mother's flesh. Eve, who has been told that she was created from a disposable part of the male body, touches the divine fruit and discovers the Mother Goddess. Suddenly she realizes that she is not less than man, shaped as an afterthought according to his need for a subdued and dutiful helpmeet. She has been made in the image of the Divine Mother. She possesses the Mother's capacity for power, sovereignty, and self-assertion. Eve bites, she chews, she takes into herself that female creative power all mention of which has been left out of the Genesis story, except for the obscure symbol of the fruit tree. This Eve, old and new at the same time, has eaten the apple of possibility. She knows what woman will become when one day she creates herself in the image of a goddess.

There were such women in Kaahumanu's time. Six feet tall, wide as possible, bare chested and magnificent. I love to think about the missionaries catching sight of them when they came to convert the Hawaiian people to Christianity. What did they think of Kaahumanu, who would swim over to visit them and stride proudly from the water, fully naked? Did they remember Eve, who had once been naked in the garden? Did they compare the radical nature of the two women? Sensing in both a subversive possibility in being female? We do not know whether a Hawaiian snake inspired Kaahumanu to eat the prohibited banana, or whether she was egged on by something restless and rebellious in herself. But I like to imagine that Kaahumanu, a huge and majestic woman, the ideal Hawaiian beauty, drew heavily upon the figure of Pele, the volcano goddess, whose fire was said to regenerate the soul.

As for Eve and her apple goddess: I shall have more to say about her as we go along and about the snake that tempts us into knowledge, and more, too, about the type of creative enterprise unleashed by one bite of the forbidden fruit. For now, I introduce the goddess in all her mystery and promise.

Carl Olsen writes: "The figure of the Goddess as represented in religious history often stands in sharp contrast to the mistaken concept that the feminine is tranquil, passive or inferior. The Goddess is associated with life-giving powers, renewal, rebirth, transformation and the mystery of death. She also attracts us with her alluring charms, arouses our curiosity about her powers and tempts us with her pleasureful and unbridled nature."

The goddess returns to a culture when women need an empowering image to guide their development. She kicks over centuries of forgetting, brings back a lost possibility of female power, lives without shame in the female body. She is the fullest possible expression of the female potential for development.

As creator of the universe, she is required by the female psyche when it dares to know itself as something fundamentally other and different from what it has been taught to be. She rises from the female side of things, out of our inborn potential as women, wipes the earth from her shoulders, looks over with a tender sort of knowing look at the Father God, wondering how he managed to get away with it all these years. For she, according to the oldest stories ever told, is his mother—creator of life, world, divinities.

As Mother Goddess, she presides over our rebirth as women. Since we do not yet know what the woman of the future might be, we require the primordial Goddess, ancient representation of female possibility. It is she who loves the girl-child created in her image and sends the snake to remind her of the goddess-fruit, from which we are expected to take a good, healthy bite. Because we seem to be afraid of eating, she asks Eve to enact this journey to the forbidden fruit, which holds within itself the knowledge of female abundance we need to incorporate if we are to get on with this work of inventing ourselves.

Born in a patriarchal garden, Eve still knows enough to pay attention to dreams and listen to animals when they come by to chat. We have forgotten that dreams bring guidance, snakes wisdom. Therefore, we are in need of an initiation that has the potential to change us fundamentally. Called by the name of women, we must still create ourselves as women.

Eve also created a new woman, as we shall see. In our contemporary reliving of that tale, the woman who will emerge from us is as yet unknown. But she is there, waiting for us to call her up out of the good, dark earth of our possibilities. This is a visionary moment, as all creation must be. There we are, kneeling down in the dirt, shaping a female with as many breasts and arms as will be required for her to step out into a world not yet ready to receive her. Yes, she is there, waiting for us to breathe life into her.

REINVENTING
EVE

Part One

INITIATION

This self-betrayal of women always struck me as a mistake, an error.

—MARGUERITE DURAS
The Lover

I

My mother used to say: "Behind every story is another story." And then she'd sit right down, wherever she was, to tell it. I've promised to tell a story about Eve in the Garden of Eden. Without doubt I'll get to it. But here, right at the beginning, I think it best to tell how I came to be thinking about the future of woman.

During my middle twenties I began to feel that I needed to tell some new kind of story. I was looking around for a myth and a mythic heroine to help in this task. In retrospect, I see the years during which I was looking for Eve as a period of initiation. I had to be pried away from my allegiance to rationality and logic, from my tendency to identify with the male heroes in the novels I read, from my pride in being able (it was said of me) to hold my own intellectually with men, which meant talking and thinking in the way they find most comfortable. It took me a long time to meet Eve because I was afraid to lose what I then regarded as my principal achievement. I was a woman who had learned how to reason abstractly. I did not want to surrender to an experience guided by strong feeling and intuitive promptings, both of which I associated in a contemptuous and disparaging way with women. Eve is the woman who sees the temptation for the opportunity it is, surrenders to the snake, sets right out on a wisdom journey. I was slower getting under way.

I recall a day in the winter of 1965. I was living in Ireland. I had driven from Dublin up into the mountains, feeling depressed and despondent. I took no pleasure in my studies, was bored and restless during serious conversations with my friends.

Looking back, I recognize this urgent dissatisfaction as the beginning of initiation. It is a time of dislocation. One grows tired of one's favorite food, can't sleep at night, gives up on the books and music one loves best, loses interest in even the oldest and most loyal obsessions, stands up suddenly in the midst of conversations, walks about by oneself, writes down scraps of thought on scraps of paper, looks for counsel in familiar places, hears nothing worth listening to, frowns, alienates friends, eats too much or stops eating much at all, feels dreadfully tired and sick of it all and at the same time as if one were in a state of unbearable suspense, waiting for the phone to ring, for the mail to arrive, for that stranger to walk around the corner. And meanwhile nothing happens and everything is just about to happen and you are, you think, too old for this sort of thing and then the despondency starts to grow and the anxiety becomes more acute and you know you're up against it, whatever it is. You can't turn back. Have you gone forward? You can't go forward. Where is there to go?

It was a cold day, I remember clearly. There was frost on the ground. Up in the mountains the trees were covered with a thin coating of ice. I was on my way to a spot my friends and I visited frequently, where we would go for picnics and drink stout and wrap ourselves in blankets and shiver, even in summer, in the cold. To get there, we had always driven past the Powerscourt estate but we had never stopped to visit. This time I stopped. I pulled over to the right and got out of the car, stamping my feet, slapping my hands against my thighs.

An old man came out of the gatehouse; he was surprised to see me, touched his finger to his cap, showed me the bell on the gate. A scrappy dog growled and came toward me, tugging at his rope. I had several cookies in my pocket. I threw one to him. He jumped up and caught it in the air, his stump of a tail wagging furiously. The gate swung back a few feet; I walked through and turned to wave at the old man, who locked it behind me.

So there I was, a visitor to the Powerscourt estate, locked in until I rang the bell and threw cookies to the dog to make my way out again. Well, why not? This is why not. From the moment the old man disappeared into the gatehouse again I felt a panic of loneliness, as if I'd been left alone in a world of strangers. I wanted to run back to the car and head out for Dublin, but I was ashamed to face the old man again.

The road was smooth and level; it was kept free of rocks and ran along a slight incline on which trees were densely planted. Their leaves had turned yellow but had not dropped from the branches. They seemed strange and otherworldly but I kept looking at them with a childlike curiosity. Whenever the breeze rose the leaves chimed together and made a desolate, frozen rattle.

Then, from out of my panic and despondency, there came an odd sensation. I felt as if I were a small girl, with little hands and legs. My entire body surged with delight, as if it had just discovered the pleasure of being a body. I jumped a fallen tree, climbed a rock, leaped down again, ran on. Soon, I came upon a flock of black sheep, grazing below me near a cluster of trees. There was not a single white sheep among them. All around me the colors were growing deeper and richer, the air was saturated with light. The flock of black sheep seemed to be grazing joyfully upon a grass so vibrant I could scarcely believe it was a material substance. Then I noticed the gray stones scattered about here and there in the field; they, too, were vibrating and pulsing with the same kind of intensity. "They're alive," I gasped. Nature, which I'd always imagined a brute dead stuff, had some kind of vivid life to it.

I had by then reached the valley's farthest edge. With every step I took, I was intending to go back. There was something uncanny in the place, bringing out something weird in me. I did not want to think that stones were alive. I did not want the logical categories through which I ordered the world to break down and desert me. I was addicted to what I then called rationality—to holding the world view the men of my time thought most plausible. Humans had consciousness and spirit and feelings. Trees and stones and sheep did not. I wanted to get out of anyplace that was teaching me anything else.

But then I noticed a waterfall pouring down a steep rock face that dropped precipitously into the river and I was running toward it. Below me was a rock pool, churning and foaming with a peculiar gleefulness. I stood there laughing back at it and then, all at once, I had the strong desire to throw off my clothes and immerse myself in the pool. I looked around me. The valley was deserted. The sheep grazed quietly; from the distance I heard the rattle from the frozen leaves. "Do it, do it," something in me kept urging, from a child's sense of delight in what should not be done. But who had decided what was and was not permitted? Here I was, a woman of the twentieth century, capable of making my own way in the world, presumably liberated, but in reality chained by unquestioned assumptions about the way thinking was to take place and the world was to be experienced and I, myself, was to behave.

I turned back toward the valley. Light was pouring down over the black sheep and the green fields as if someone had just lifted a bucket and were watering everything in sight. I looked up and saw that this light was flooding down from a sky that was not any longer a sky. It was, as I looked, withdrawing behind shimmering veils of blue light. And now the whole valley became one great wave of light, rising and falling, shaping and dissolving. My idea that the sky was a sky and the tree a tree, separate and distinguishable from one another, had to be questioned. Here they were dissolving into one another. Was it possible everything I had been told about the universe was simply an assumption, a style of perception, rather than truth?

It was too late to flee from the place. I, the rationalist, was in the grip of extreme emotion. I could fight it off, run away, or surrender and find out what it meant. I found myself before an immense tree. Near the bottom it had been split almost in two by lightning and in the charred, concave base, a brilliant green-and-yellow lichen was growing. I stared at the tree, a natural altar. I wondered, had the Druids worshipped this tree? I tried to distract myself with this thought and meanwhile my body was doing something peculiar. I noticed it, thought I should fight it, was doing it anyway. Then it was done. There I was, on the ground in front of the tree. Tears streaming down my face. I, raised in a family of Marxist atheists, down on my knees, worshipping?

II

The story of Alice Koller. At the age of thirty-seven she looks into the mirror one morning and discovers the same feeling I, too, had when living in Ireland. "I stare into the mirror," she writes in *An Unknown Woman*. "I don't have a life, I'm just using up a number of days somehow. There is no REASON for me to be here. No plan formulated at some point in the past has led me to this void that is my day, every day . . ."

She, too, has been leading the typical life of the "liberated" woman in our culture, moving about from city to city, preoccupied by her relationships with men. She has a doctorate, hasn't decided yet for what she wants to use it. She is exhausted. "I'm tired, from the inside out. Tired of perpetually having to fight for everything: degree, men, jobs, money. Tired of running after things that always elude me."

Alice Koller acts. She makes an impulsive decision to give up the life she has been living and find a place for solitude. It isn't the first time the idea has occurred to her. But this time she won't let herself be stopped because she has no money. She sits down, trembling. But she has found a goal that is her own, "a focus for the long minutes of my day. I will get money, and then I will go away."

At a similar moment in my own life I, too, "went away." I drove off the road I had traveled with my friends and discovered a solitary valley where I dared meet up with an overwhelming emotion. It marked my life with a radical departure. After that walk I would never again be able to take anything for granted about myself or my perception of the world. Driving back down to Dublin from the mountains I felt like a shell that had no egg inside it. I was hollow where a self should be. Never had I allowed myself to have a spontaneous, idiosyncratic response to the world. But let me go off just once alone and I was invaded by impulses, sensations, perceptions, that seemed fundamentally at odds with what I had been taught to be. I was frightened, hunching forward in the seat to peer through the fogged-up glass. When I knelt down before the burnt-out tree a real person had known a genuine emotion. Was it possible, I wondered, that I had never until then experienced myself authentically?

Alice Koller goes to Nantucket. She buys a pup, drives to the ferry, crosses to the winter isle of self-chosen initiation, and there, in spite of loneliness, the winds, isolation, and the terrors of solitude, she begins the quest for knowledge. "The case is the same, and I must not forget it: everything preceding Nantucket has been a horror, and may be so again, if there is an again, unless I force out all the truth there is in me." That move was for her, as the next years of my life would be for me, a journey of self-discovery, during which she asked herself to shatter the habitual patterns by which she had been confined so that she could discover the truth of herself as a woman.

"I'm fighting to break out of a pattern of what I've been doing for, my God, twenty-four years. A quarter of a century, a third of a lifetime. I haven't got twenty-four years to undo the pattern slowly, I have to smash its hold as fast as I can. Each thing I do during the course of a day is something I've been told to do, or taught to do. I have to replace all of it with what I choose to do."

Other women, other stories. They all begin with a despair grown suddenly raucous, a feeling that something long ignored has announced itself finally, demanding attention. Suddenly, out of nowhere, a woman finds herself doing things she'd never believed possible and then, when it's all over, she can scarcely believe she stopped her car on the way to work, walked out over the mud flats where the driftwood gathers, tied together with shredded bits from her stockings a driftwood skeleton with a lipstick sign in its hands: I RESIGN.

Her name is Eleanor. She did not go to work that day; for the week following she called in sick. She spent the next months in a state of conflict. She grew preoccupied with food, began to grind her own flour and bake whole-grain bread, lost weight, sought purity in a comestible form, grew gaunt and skeletal. At last she reached a decision. She rented out her large flat in the Berkeley hills and moved to a small cottage on the coast. Her law partners probably never glimpsed the skeleton with the lipstick sign in her formal letter of resignation. But it was there.

In her run-down shack, without indoor plumbing, she continues to bake, loses more weight, sells breads and cookies to the grocery in the neighboring town, keeps a diary, spends the mornings in bed. "During the first two months the only discovery I made was the fact that I wasn't there, there simply wasn't any me to get itself up in the morning and find a purpose in the day." A sense of self, that came slowly.

"In the beginning I stayed in bed until noon, cowering under the covers, reading books that no longer meant anything to me. Then one day, I was coming back from town and I saw a patch of violet gentians growing along the road. I don't know why, but for some reason I stopped my car and got out to look at them. There they were, perfectly ordinary flowers growing in small clusters, but I stood there staring at them as if someone had just opened the book of my life to the right page. 'Yes,' I thought, that's it. I'll plant a garden.' "

There are no happy endings here, no endings whatever. Alice Koller leaves Nantucket after four months and knows only that she is on her way. But she has looked into her life, called up memory, relived the past, faced suicide, taken apart the rules that confined her, discovered a self with its own wants and desires. The future is blank, an empty page in an open book. But the pen is in her hand and that hand belongs now to a woman who has freed herself of what she has been taught to be.

The woman who plants a garden is still living in her cottage on the coast. She has never installed a telephone there; a few years ago she used to call me once a week to speak for an hour from the public telephone outside the post office. These days she gets up early to tend her garden; she has gained weight and has assembled a vast library of diaries written by women. At night the moths flutter around her oil lamp as she lies on the floor in front of the fire, asking questions. Asking questions . . .

A woman is in the kitchen, wearing an apron. She is preparing a beef Wellington for a formal dinner. She has cooked the beef with shallots and onions and wine. She spreads it with homemade chicken liver pâté. She rolls out the dough, sets the beef down on it, and then suddenly, working very methodically, she shapes the dough as a pig. Yes, there it is, ready for baking, a porcine beef Wellington for a formal dinner. Years later, she discovers from her reading that the pig in ancient times had been the sacred animal of the Vegetation Goddess.

"I wouldn't want to tell you that the beef Wellington changed my life. But, on the other hand, why not? You have to date these things from some point, don't you? Or maybe it was that dinner party. That silence when I finally carried that pig-shaped beef into the living room. That must have been it, that moment when I didn't apologize and didn't explain. I just stood there, my hands folded in front of me, as Jack made some awkward joke about my 'creativity,' stood up quickly, and cut into the dough. No great drama. But something happened after that, it happened inside me . . ."

An impulse that turns a beef Wellington into a pig. A glance at the mirror into a moment of truth. A drive along the freeway into a gesture of protest. Impulses of this kind are irresistible and that's as it should be, for they are bringing to the surface inclinations that have long been buried and feared. One wishes to spend more time alone, becomes far more selective about one's friends, grows to dislike dinner parties, discovers long nature walks, pays a fortune for a pair of binoculars, spends an entire morning, when one should have been preparing a term paper, or a brief, or a beef Wellington, crouched down on one's haunches on the hill above the lake watching the mating rituals of the red-winged blackbirds.

We are foraging for a self, some first knowing what a woman might be when she has stripped away the rules that have bound her in and made her tame enough for the father-culture. "Know thyself"—that was the ancient wisdom of the Delphic oracle, a woman of inspired knowledge. "Plant wildflowers, sow seeds in the wind"—that is what the oracle might tell us today. We are a domesticated species and we need to take back the wildness that is in us.

I didn't go to Nantucket for my journey of self-discovery or up the north coast to a little cottage in the woods. I never made a beef Wellington into a pig as a declaration of freedom. I made a solitary winter island of my life, withdrawing from my friends, giving up my job teaching children in the Hebrew day school. I had dropped out of graduate school with some vague sense that I was intended by "destiny" to do something meaningful with my life. So far I hadn't found out what that was supposed to be. I was spending more than I earned, was close to the bottom of my small savings, didn't know how to make a living. I was in my twenties, divorced, raising a little girl, mooning about all over San Francisco with my hands in my pockets.

"Mama," my daughter would say, crawling into bed with me, and something inside me would snap into place, as if the last remaining shred of order in my personality had organized itself instinctively. Then we'd start our usual race to see who could get dressed first. She in the blue uniform for the French-American bilingual school. I in my equally mandatory uniform: faded Levi's, heavy sweater, tennis shoes, navy-blue jacket from the surplus store on Market Street. It didn't occur to me that I, too, was getting dressed for school, but in retrospect I see it clearly. Nature had become a schoolroom for me. Years before, I had been drawn to my knees before a burnt-out tree. I still did not know why. But now I turned back to the pools and mountains. Here I was free to be myself. To strip off my clothes and bathe in a woodland pool. To climb trees, watch the birds, lie down in a clearing, dissolve into an aching kinship with grass and earth. Each day, in spite of anxiety and depression, the minute I had dropped my daughter off at school I'd head for the Golden Gate Park or drive across the bridge to Mt. Tamalpais or go over to Berkeley and climb up into the hills. Something was taking shape within me. Eventually I understood it as a longing to peel back layer after layer of pretense, compliance, and accommodation so that I could stand naked before myself as a woman.

I resisted acknowledging this desire for a long time. But gradually, as I found myself out of doors in the rain, standing bare-headed in my garden before dawn and after midnight, I began to admit that I had been drawn out of my house by a wish to disinvent myself as patriarchal female, to give myself back to the nature that was in me, grow profusely, overstep my bounds, step out of the confined plot to which I had been assigned, and finally admit, in the most radical possible way, that I as a woman did not exist.

It wasn't a question of taking a degree, finding a profession, getting to work. This idea, which had seemed radical enough until then, did not have much to recommend it now. Why should I want to become what the men around me already were? I did not know a single man who lived with passion, risked being absurd, stripped off his clothes to immerse himself in nature, wept in awe at a tree.

My intellect had been developed by male teachers and writers who thought about the world in a way that reflected their experience of it. My sexuality had been organized by Hollywood movies and Madison Avenue advertising campaigns. My idea of what a woman is and could be was derived from a society that had a recurrent need to insist on my inferiority and spent a great deal of its time and culture keeping me down. The more I thought about myself as a woman the less of me there seemed to be.

But if I tore down all preordained assumptions about the nature of myself as woman, what would I be? Selfless in the most severe sense of the word. A woman with no self, facing the female void. "We are the hollow men," T. S. Eliot had written. "Headpiece filled with straw." But for women the situation was even worse. This straw with which we had been stuffed wasn't even our straw. Woman, keeping to her place in patriarchal culture, was nothing more than an accumulated terror, a blind fear of what we might become if we dared, just once, create ourselves.

How could I imagine there was hidden knowledge, old memory, another possibility of being female? I knew that I experienced an intense claustrophobia within the confined world of my life, that when I was out in nature something stirred, awakened, seemed riotous, wanted to run wild. Perhaps the birds flying over my head were shaped as an omen? Perhaps this life I was living was a brief moment in a long, unending series. Men might die with the death of the body. Maybe women didn't?

At times, walking about among the trees, I had the distinct impression they were aware of my rootless wandering and regarded me as a creature similar to themselves. In the redwood grove, where I lay for hours staring up into the sky, there were trees that had begun to grow in the time of Caesar. Maybe I was about to remember myself as a sapling, putting out first shoots?

Initiation is not a predictable process. It moves forward fitfully, through moments of clear seeing, dramatic episodes of feeling, subtle intuitions, vague contemplative states. Dreams arrive, bringing guidance we frequently cannot accept. Years pass, during which we know that we are involved in something that cannot be easily named. We wake to a sense of confusion, know that we are in dangerous conflict, cannot define the nature of what troubles us. All change is like this. It circles around, snakes back on itself, finds detours, leads us a merry chase, starts us out it seems all over again from where we were in the first place. And then suddenly, when we least expect it, something opens a door, discovers a threshold, shoves us across.

Hiking boots appear on the feet of a woman used to wearing heels. An acquaintance shows up for coffee one afternoon with a pair of binoculars around her neck. We see old friends in the vegetable store or in the long lines at the bakery. We detect the light in their eyes of eyes that have begun to look inward. We notice fingernails not quite freed of clay, hands with something of the soil about them or those fine cuts where a nail or a saw or the edge of a hammer has touched their skin, and we imagine of them, these women who have called us less often lately, that they, too, have been touched by solitude. And so we come to know, listening to women talking to one another on the bus, after the trial, before the patients arrive for the day, in the car pool, in the grocery store, at the swimming pool, in the coffee shop, at the Coke machine, in the lunchroom, that everywhere, all over this land, women are beginning to discover, through little moments of knowing and through dramatic revelations, another sense of what it means to be a woman.

III

Recently I came across a remarkable diary. It was written by Etty Hillesum, a young Jewish woman living in Holland during the Holocaust years. Etty started out a rational person, as I, too, had done. But she had strong moods, a frequent sense of inner chaos; she was passionate, thoughtful, deeply introspective, took long walks, and kept a diary. She had a greed for food and began to wonder about the symbolic meaning of her hunger. That was in 1941.

> And while I ostensibly ponder problems of ethics and truth and God Himself, I have developed an 'eating problem.' . . . I know I have to watch myself but I am sometimes seized by a greed so powerful that it brooks no argument. I am convinced that this eating problem can be rooted out. Ultimately, it is purely symbolic. . . . And it will probably turn out to have some connection with my dear Mama.

Reading Etty, I found myself wishing I could have made her acquaintance twenty years earlier. I might then have known another woman who transformed a hunger for food into a spiritual quest. Etty made use of the word *God.* Then she began to subvert its traditional sense and to find God in places only a woman might look. To begin with, I, too, thought my longing to know myself was a desire for divine guidance. But the help I needed could not come from Holy Writ or any mediated authority. I needed to claim the authority of my own experience, to trust the wisdom of my body. I needed a story about a woman who creates the world from her own substance. I needed a cultural tradition in which women had the universe at their breasts, gave suck to gods and mortals, decided how things should be, had some say in them. I needed a someone who had been there from the beginning sticking up for the female side of things. I needed a goddess.

I had no idea that I was looking for an embodied image of female potential when I went out on my walks. But I had begun to lose my fear of the wildness called up in me by wild, uncultivated places. Gradually I came to sense the trees and lakes and wildflowers as a nurturant power. Wandering about in the rose garden one day I had the impression there was a presence in the garden. It seemed to be all around me, trying to get my attention. I could not see or touch it, but this time, as I was drawn to my knees, I felt that I was held against the breast of nature.

As these experiences grew more familiar I began to make associations between them and certain changes in my body. When my menstrual periods began with the full moon I would be particularly open to episodes of ineffable meaning. On the days before my blood I would be restless and moody, inclined to weep and despair and to wonder where my rootless existence was leading. But then, as the moon grew full, I would have a sense of power shaping itself in me, too.

Etty, in her day, was also making connections

> between certain moods and menstruation . . . Yesterday evening I was certainly flying high. And tonight it is suddenly as if my blood stream has been transformed. Life feels altogether different . . . I used to think: I don't want any children, so why must I go through this senseless monthly performance . . . And in a rash and pleasure-loving moment

I thought of having my womb removed. But you have to accept yourself as you were created . . . The interaction of body and soul is a most mysterious thing. The remarkable, dreamy and yet illuminating mood I was in last night and this morning was due to this very change in my body.

Etty Hillesum's diary records the same highly dramatic initiation into female experience I, too, would know a quarter of a century later. For her, too, this process involved a gradual awakening to nature.

I went to bed early last night and from my bed I stared out through the large open window. And it was once more as if life with all its mysteries was close to me, as if I could touch it. I had the feeling that I was resting against the naked breast of life, and could feel her gentle and regular heartbeat. I felt safe and protected. And I thought: how strange. It is wartime. There are concentration camps . . . And yet, at unguarded moments, when left to myself, I suddenly lie against the naked breast of life and her arms around me are so gentle and so protective . . .

In February 1941, the first antipogrom demonstration in European history took place in Amsterdam. In response, the Nazis stepped up the Jewish persecution. Jews were deprived of jobs, forbidden to shop in non-Jewish stores, enclosed in ghettos, sent to work camps. In March 1941 Etty Hillesum began her diary. It was wartime; there were concentration camps. And yet, Etty risked madness, in order to reclaim a self.

She writes:

Yesterday morning, running about in the mist, once again that feeling: I have truly reached my limits, everything has happened before . . . I can go no further than I have already gone, the frontiers are too close and to cross them means making straight for a mental institution. Or for death?

This reaching of limits changes Etty. She has been the predictable, token female, to whom everything has already happened. Cultured, worldly, proudly intellectual, she is as much like a man as she can possibly be. Then she crosses the border of the patriarchal frontier and finds, not madness, but her own vision and truth.

> There is a sort of lamentation and loving-kindness as well as a little wisdom inside me that cry to be let out. Sometimes several different dialogues run through me at the same time, images and figures, moods, a sudden flash of something that must be my very own truth . . . And there is God. The girl who could not kneel but learned to do so on the rough coconut matting in an untidy bathroom. Such things are often more intimate than sex. The story of the girl who gradually learned to kneel is something I would love to write in the fullest possible way.

Etty never stopped using the word *God*. But she was gradually drawn to claim the authority of her own experience. Then she transposed God into herself.

> When I pray I hold a silly, naive or deadly serious dialogue with what is deepest inside me, which for convenience sake I call God . . . And that probably best expresses my feeling for life: I repose in myself. And that part of myself, that deepest and richest part in which I repose, is what I call "God."

In July 1942, the first major street roundup of Jews occurred in Amsterdam, where Etty was working for the Jewish Council. With a special permit from the Council, Etty was allowed to go back and forth a dozen times between Amsterdam and Westerbork, the transit camp that was the last stop on the way to Auschwitz. Ill herself at the time, she carried letters, messages, contacted resistance groups, brought back medicines. A few months later she wrote in her diary about the poet Rilke, who had inspired her, that someone so frail, "who did most of his writing behind protective walls, would have been broken in the circumstances in which we live." About herself in Westerbork she wrote: "Those two months behind barbed wire have been the two richest and most intense months of my life, in which my highest values were deeply confirmed."

The story of the girl who learned to kneel began, as we first encounter it in her diaries, with "mortal fear in every fibre. Complete collapse. Lack of self-confidence. Aversion. Panic."

It moved on to a clear seeing of the world around her. "Very well then, this new certainty, that what they are after is our total destruction, I accept it. I know it now and I shall not burden others with my fears."

It ended in affirmation. On August 18, 1943, Etty wrote from Westerbork:

> You have made me so rich, oh God . . . Sometimes when I stand in some corner of the camp, my feet planted on Your earth, my eyes raised towards Your Heaven, tears sometimes run down my face, tears of deep emotion and gratitude . . . The beat of my heart has grown deeper, more active and yet more peaceful, and it is as if I were all the time storing up inner riches.

Etty, who could have gone into hiding in Amsterdam, refused to accept the help and advice of her friends. She had volunteered to accompany the first group of Jews sent to Westerbork camp. Finally, refusing to let her friends kidnap her from Westerbork, she accompanied her family to the death camp. Farmers found a postcard Etty had thrown from the train on the way to Auschwitz: "We have left the camp singing."

Two years later a remarkable archaeological discovery

was made in Nag Hammadi in Upper Egypt. While gathering a soft soil used for the fertilization of crops, an Arab peasant named Muhammad Ali al-Samman found a red earthenware jar. He smashed the jar and discovered inside it thirteen papyrus books, bound in leather. Elaine Pagels has written about these extraordinary books, which eventually became known to the world as the Gnostic Gospels. They contained "some fifty-two texts from the early centuries of the Christian Era—including a collection of early Christian gospels, previously unknown." From the papyrus in the leather bindings and from the Coptic script used in the texts, they can be dated with little debate from c. A.D. 350–400. But the original teachings, from which the fifty-two texts found in Nag Hammadi were taken, have been dated by some scholars as early as the second century after Christ and are considered by others to include "traditions even *older* than the New Testament."

We shall hear more about these gospels, which were circulated at the beginning of the Christian Era and were suppressed as banned documents during a struggle critical for the formation of early Christianity. Here, it will be sufficient to take note of certain extremely unusual tendencies in these texts, which tell a curious tale about the beginning of the human race. For these texts, buried for almost two thousand years, contain myths and poems and secret teachings that speak of a divine feminine power and regard the snake as the principle of divine wisdom.

Etty Hillesum died in Auschwitz in November 1943. She knew nothing about the Gnostic Gospels and their buried tradition of goddess worship. But her experience at the core of herself had awakened her buried powers. In the face of death, surrounded by barbed wire, the deportation and destruction of her people, she had thrown herself upon the naked breast of life and had drawn from this event the courage to know God as a woman—her own gesture of self-repose.

Is it possible then? The female God is coming back to the world after thousands of years of suppression by the father-culture? She is breaking through the earth of her actual burial? Unearthing herself from the female psyche? Making a claim to us? Taking us by the hair? Calling out when we try to ignore her? Bringing us to our knees? Can it be that the initiation process occurring among women today is part of an historic moment in which the Great Goddess of the ancient world is hastening back to redress the patriarchal imbalance in our culture? If so, initiation must be the meeting place of self with history, the spiritual with the political, the intensely personal with the power relations of a troubled world. When a woman seriously asks herself what it means to be a woman she is pulling at a thread that can unravel an entire culture.

IV

Knowledge of the feminine divine principle existed long before the Gnostic Gospels were unearthed. Mythologists had studied the prominence of the Great Mother in the stories told about the universe in ancient cultures. She had aroused debate and controversy during the middle of the nineteenth century, when scholars speculated about the type of society in which the Great Mother was worshipped. She had been dug up out of the earth before, in Willendorf, Lespugne, Menton, Lausel, a figurine with protruding abdomen and enormous breasts. But the most abundant evidence of her existence has been unearthed in the years since the war, as archaeologists have uncovered the ruins of the Old and New Stone Age cultures. During the forty-odd years since the Gnostic Gospels were discovered, in the last year of the war, hundreds of statues and figurines of the Great Mother have been emerging, after thousands of years of burial.

Digging down, cutting through layers, delving deep, uncovering: that is what it takes to find her. She has rested there in her earth womb, ready for rebirth these thousands of years.

Who is this ancient Goddess?

Archaeology says: she was worshipped for more than twenty thousand years, from the Paleolithic era to the Neolithic, in "various places within a vast arc covering the Russian Steppes, the Indus Valley and Western Asia, and the Mediterranean Basin, as well as Western and Central Europe."

She belonged to the pre-Indo-European civilization of Old Europe, in which soil was tended and time moved slowly; a culture ". . . . characterized by a dominance of woman in society and worship of a Goddess incarnating the creative principle as Source and Giver of All."

It is a time of slow and irregular advances in agriculture and the making of artifacts. Wheat and barley grow up in cultivated fields; the sun rises; goats, sheep, pigs, and cattle are domesticated; the sun sets; clay is shaped and fired, stone tools polished in the self-sustaining villages that have risen up out of the temporary Mesolithic campsites of the wandering peoples who had gathered nuts, harvested wild wheat, and hunted the bison. Peaceful, sedentary, slowly changing. Men go to live in the woman's village when they marry. Children derive their descent from the mother. Women and men worship the Goddess.

And then something happened. It upset this peaceful life that had begun to use copper and gold for tools and ornamentation. Something took place. It changed beyond recognition this village life that had begun to create townships, where crafts had become more highly specialized, religious and governmental institutions had emerged, rudimentary scripts developed. Suddenly, with great violence, moving quickly, bringing a whole new sense of time into this sedentary life, another order of civilization appeared. It came down upon Europe in the course of three waves of infiltration from the Russian Steppes. This was Indo-European culture. It swept down, it raced over, it overturned, it conquered, it brought the father gods, great warrior deities of its invasion. The archaeologist Maria Gimbutas, speaking calmly and with objectivity, says: "The female deities, or more accurately the Goddess Creatrix in her many aspects, were largely replaced by the predominantly male divinities of the Indo-Europeans." And we imagine the centuries of warfare evoked by these words, the patriarchal hordes from the Russian Steppes sweeping down upon the peaceful villages of the mother-culture, burning and raping, looting and destroying.

Who was this Goddess?

The earth, giving her back to us, says:

She was mistress of the waters: bird, snake, crane, goose, duck, staring back at us from a vase, eyes all-seeing as rain falls below her from beyond clouds where primordial waters lie.

She brings the waters of renewal.

The spade strikes her, the hand brushes away dirt. She emerges from the ground: the Neolithic Virgin, holding her hands to her breasts. She is sitting there, supported by leopards. Goddess of Life, Death, and Regeneration.

She brings back another sense of what it means to be female.

She wears a mask, she sits on a throne from a Vinca site; she was buried sometime during the mid-fifth millennium before the birth of Christ. The domesticated dog, the bull, and the he-goat are her companions. She rules both wild and cultivated life.

She reminds us, there is wildness in us.

She is the pregnant goddess with a snake winding about her belly. She is bottle-shaped, pillar-headed; the snake winds twice above her abdomen.

She brings rebirth.

She is a forgotten possibility of female power. She returns to us now, thrusting herself out of the earth. She brings memories of a time so old we had almost forgotten it, except for the old stories. She asks us to remember what a woman might be like, unearthing her old powers. This is what she means by healing.

Who is this Goddess?

The stories say:

She was Isis, born from the swamps of the Nile, keeping a watchful eye on earth's people; she taught them to grind, to bake, to spin, to weave, to pot.

She lets us know: we, too, have created civilization.

She was Anat, Anata, Anath, Anit, Anta: Great Goddess of Ugarit. Warrior, mother, virgin, and wanton. Worshipped for her ecstasy.

She brings desire.

She was Ishtar, Ashdar, Astar, Istar, and Istaru, ". . . the mother holding her massive breasts, symbols of her benevolence. She was judge and counselor, the old wise one whom women emulated in the courts and the homes of her land."

She is female wisdom, benevolent power.

Anatu, ruler of earth and sky, Ishtar's mother.

Ambika: "little mother," goddess of death, Kali.

Amalthea: magical nanny goat. Zeus was fed from her by Adamanthea, his Cretan nurse.

She is Tlazolteotl, "dirty lady," "earth's heart," Aztec goddess of the fourfold moon, witch-goddess of sexuality and license.

She is Toci, "our grandmother." She wears a skirt of shells, carries the sun disk on her shield.

She brings healing.

She is Ymoja, sister of the fishes, river mother of spirits hailing from West Africa; Goddess of women, we bring her yams and fowls and get children from her in return.

She presides over the birth of the Woman Who Is Not Yet.

We learn to tell her old stories:

The story of Gula, who watered the great tree in the garden at the center of the earth. Mother goddess, "great physician," able to cure and to inflict disease. Gula, who plucked the fruit from the tree to offer to her worshippers. Who is this Goddess? She is ancient; she is widespread; she gives birth to life, she eats up death; she has the eyes of wisdom, she is fertile, she knows what there is to know, gives her children fruit to eat, feeds them power at her breast. She lives deep-buried in that richest part of the self where a woman finds repose. She was worshipped, she has been forgotten. During the years since the war she has returned to us. From the earth.

From the village of Anzabegovo in southeast Yugoslavia. Excavated in 1960. The Great Mother, who heals.

From the village of Agrissa, Thessaly, Greece. Excavated 1955–58. The Great Mother, who restores.

From Azmak, Central Bulgaria, excavated 1960–63. The Great Mother, who reminds us.

From Cernavoda, a cemetery site of the Hamangia culture. Excavated 1957. The Great Mother, who inspires.

From Gorza, in southeastern Hungary. Excavated 1956–63. The goddess of possibility.

From Nag Hammadi, in Egypt. In 1945. The Gnostic Gospels, in which the Goddess still exists.

She had been known and worshipped far more recently than we had supposed—within our own culture and by one of the two major religions that had shaped it. We discover: her power over human imagination had lasted long beyond the Neolithic villages in their peaceful brooding and slow evolving. She must have survived in the old stories told at the village well, in the ritual bath, by women walking to the temple, gathering herbs for drying, beating their clothes against the rocks along the river. She was still there in the years early Christianity was creating itself. And now her voice spoke out again in 1945 from a tractate of the Gnostic Gospels, proclaiming her "absolute transcendence . . . whose greatness is incomprehensible and whose being is unfathomable." A female divine presence. She says:

> For I am knowledge and ignorance
> I am shame and boldness
> I am shameless; I am ashamed
> I am strength and I am fear
> I am war and peace.
> Give heed to me
> I am the one who is disgraced and the great one.

This is the female presence who brings the reconciliation of opposites; she is an image of our wholeness.

There is another story of female power in the Gnostic Gospels. In this one, a female presence wishes to experience conception through herself. She is one of the nine Muses, who withdraws to a high mountain and spends time by herself there in order to become androgynous. She succeeds. She desires herself alone, fulfills her desire, and becomes pregnant from that desire.

This is the Muse, fulfilled by her own desire, who inspires the creation of the future woman.

In one of the Gnostic scriptures, Eve creates Adam through the power of her own word. "'Adam, live,' she says, because she sees him cast down upon the ground and pities him. 'Rise up upon the earth!' Immediately her word became a deed. For when Adam rose up, immediately he opened his eyes. When he saw her, he said, 'You will be called "the mother of the living," because you are the one who gave me life.'"

This is Eve, who gives life, mother of the living, unearthed in Nag Hammadi in 1945, who has come back to guide our initiation.

V

In 1971 I went to Israel to live on a kibbutz. I was longing for regeneration through humble work. I connected this desire with *eretz Isroel.* The earth, the soil. Since I had first walked into the valley of black sheep at the Powerscourt estate, I had longed to kick back the dead leaf and uncover the true ground of myself. But with every step I took, the skeptic in me had something to say.

This skeptic, hard-edged, never innocent, born knowing, rather bitter, not likely to take the risk of believing in anything, narrowing its eyes, puffing out its chest, smiling scornfully at my "female exaggerations," had been driven against the wall and was fighting back for all it was worth. It directed its sharpest thrusts against my "mysticism, and related rot," trying to reason me out of my growing fascination with the subtle, extremely potent, as yet unnamed something I found in nature.

Every time I walked off the kibbutz, into the fields and hills that surrounded it, I responded to the landscape with a growing rapture, as if I were returning home after thousands of years of absence. The black goats grazing on the white rocks in a rust-red earth, the wild river valleys where dark-skinned women from neighboring villages tended their flocks, the purple mountains covered in mist, drawing away into the distance, all called to me from an old knowledge, demanding my surrender.

But how could I surrender?

The gossip. The woman raving. The witch. The woman who mutters beneath her breath. The woman who can't think without weeping. The woman who gathers herbs by moonlight and dries them in secret beneath her bed. The woman who claims to see what isn't there. The woman who knows the future before it happens. The woman who doesn't read the newspaper, hasn't a clue what is going on in the world, but insists that her daughter, ten thousand miles from her, is in danger. This creature, for whom we have been taught so much contempt—is she what I was becoming?

I had left my daughter in California with her father. It was painful to think of the time that would pass before I was settled enough to send for her. In fact, I never did get settled enough. I returned home ten months later. I was a different person when I got back. An arrow, spinning in circles all my life, had now pointed.

On the kibbutz I became an expert pruner of trees. I made a few friends. They came over to have tea with me in the late afternoons. But the nights were difficult; the wild mountain setting, a few yards from the Lebanese border, where the Israeli army was building a security road, did little to give me peace of mind. I was not frightened by the sound of shelling or the sudden arrival of Israeli soldiers on the track of terrorists hidden in the neighboring caves. It was, rather, the wildness of the place calling to the kindred wildness in me that unsettled my efforts to become a hard-working farmer, hands hardened by toil. In the early evenings I would climb up into the guard towers that looked down over the valley.

One day a bird swept out over the landscape. I watched it soaring and wheeling against the darkening sky. Then I noticed something remarkable. For that brief instant the world was suspended in a perfect balance. In everything there was an equal light and darkness. In the grass below me, in the purple mountains, in the piercing blue of the Mediterranean, in the taut wings of the bird. A poise. A stillness. All things divided equally between day and night, the light and the dark, the expectation and the fulfillment. It was a universe held in perfect balance, its opposites contained and reconciled. I sensed, in that image, the sudden, rapturous possibility of bringing about a state of accord between the warring parts of myself.

By the time I got back to my room I saw a lot in this idea. Reason had its place, without doubt, in what I was experiencing. Its categories had helped me give shape over the years to a highly irrational, often chaotic experience. But there were times when these categories had to be set aside so that a new perception of life could emerge. If this experience upset the neat labels that had been put upon things then it would be the work of reason to re-order its ordering principles and make them serve the exposition of intuitive truth. I would never cease to think about my experience. But I could not use reason as a way of warding off the power of rapture. That was like being forced to choose between day and night, light and darkness, the known and the unknown, as if only one of these polar opposites were real.

I lit the heater and got under the covers. That was it? As simple as that? Here, finally, was the next step I had been trying to take? Where I had previously perceived irreconcilable opposition between reason and worship, I now grasped the possibility of bringing them together. This was the lesson I had been trying to learn since Dublin. I was capable of logic, discipline, and self-control. I was capable of wild, exuberant, visionary dreaming.

A few days later I was in my room after a day of strenuous labor in the orchards. Lying in bed, I heard a voice. It said: "For it is possible to rise by joy, through those same stages of initiation suffering required."

I sat up and folded my arms around my knees. "Voices? Now she's hearing voices?" the undying skeptic in me immediately brought out. But this time instead of mocking and dismissing the voice, why not listen to it?

I went to look out the window; I opened it wide and leaned over the valley. Later, if I wanted to, I could work out some theory about subvocal, mental voices. For now, this voice had named what until then had been nameless. From the moment I had knelt down before the tree in the mountains above Dublin, I had been involved in a process of initiation.

What could I say about this experience? To begin with, it was not separate from my body. Usually it arose as my menstrual blood dropped down. Although spiritual, it did not require a mortification of the body. Furthermore, it made me capable of a particular type of thought. Since that day in Dublin I had been fascinated by questions about the nature of reality, which had not really interested me before that time. Evidently, this type of initiation asked me to overcome the conflict I had always perceived between thinking and feeling.

And then there was nature: In my early twenties I had felt myself to be outside of nature. Now I participated in it. The flow of my blood was connected to the cycles of moons and tides; a bird in flight called me into its flying. Working in the orchards I felt in need of strong roots, seasons of change. When the afternoons were hot we lay down under the apple trees to rest and I grew back into the earth, into a second body.

Moreover, over the years the initiation process had irreversibly changed my mode of perception. Now, every stone and tree I looked at seemed to have a soul, to feel and bleed, rejoice and suffer. All this I had come to understand not through reading holy books that instructed me in religious doctrine, but through my own immediate, intensely felt relationship to the universe, which I had come to know not by taking it as an object of study but through a process of identification and participation that overcame all sense of separation between what I looked at and what I became in the process of looking.

Consequently, the organizational categories I had always taken for granted had also changed over the years. One day, observing the tiny, blue, star-shaped flower that grew from a weed out of the cracked earth on the path behind the kibbutz, I had wondered why people categorized some plants as desirable and some as weeds—everything I looked at seemed to have, in that moment, the same quality of a majestic beauty. It must have been that day I first noticed the exquisite purple color of cow dung drying on the path. It, too, although it embarrassed me to think it, seemed to hold the same quality of a revealed divinity, a sense that the deepest possible meaningfulness and presence were woven into the humblest, most insignificant bits of matter. Cow dung and weeds, apple trees and black goats, the Arab boys wandering after their flocks in the dry river valley, the hawks soaring overhead, the woman crouched down on the ruins in a state of ecstatic observation—all told the same story of a divinity embedded in the human body, rising from the earth, dropping down from the sky, weaving together thinking and feeling, perceiving and being in a linked participation that gave order, meaning, and direction to life. If this experience shattered the idea of the divine as male and unknowable, if it called into question the idea of spirit as an elusive essence that hovered unattainably outside of human reach, then it was time to

give up these ideas and place myself at risk in a new relationship to the universe. Whatever I might someday become, for now this is what it meant to be a woman.

The value of such thinking was immediately apparent. It
shifted the focus of my preoccupation from theories about
experience to the experience itself. It brought to mind an
event that had occurred almost two months earlier, a few
days after I had arrived in Israel.

I had been wandering about by myself in a small village
of Moroccan Jews visible, below in the valley, from our
kibbutz. We had driven down in the late afternoon and
parked the truck discreetly out of sight, knowing that we
should not be driving. It was the evening of Yom Kippur.
Most of us had eaten a small meal in the dining room and
would not eat again until nightfall of the next day. When we
reached the village on foot the others went ahead, walking
in a purposeful stride toward the synagogue. I came along
more slowly. The village was interesting to me. It reminded
me of the small town in Russia where my mother had been
born. The same dusty streets, dilapidated houses, dogs and
chickens wandering in and out. A sense, too, of something
ancient and enduring that had managed to survive the poverty and dirt.

I lost track of my companions. The village girls, who had
not gone to temple on the holiest night of the year, came to
walk with me. At first there were only a few of them. We
walked on, the little girls trailing after me. Soon we were
joined by others, who came running toward us, delighted
by this opportunity for diversion. I provided plenty. There
I was, in a long, brightly colored dress, a shawl over my
shoulders. I looked as if I belonged somewhere ethnic but
I was unable to speak a word to them. My only Hebrew
was the absurd phrase that I could not speak Hebrew. This

set them off into wild laughter; after all, there I was, speaking it.

They tried again and again, chattering at me, pointing to themselves, pointing to the kibbutz on the mountain, running around me in circles. I would listen intently to what they were saying, hesitate for a moment when they had finished talking. Then, as they waited with great anticipation, standing up on their tiptoes, their eyes wide, mouths open, sucking in their breath, I did it again. No, nothing had changed: I still had only my one phrase. I could not speak Hebrew.

Eventually they must have decided that I was not playing a game. They began to look at me with a serious compassion. Finally, overcoming their shyness, they drew close and took charge of me. They crowded around me, grabbed my skirt; they went on chattering at me in Hebrew and kept right on laughing when I couldn't chatter back. Then I had an inspiration. I knelt down in the dust. I put my arms around them and told them my name. That much at least I had learned in Hebrew class. *"Ani Kim,"* I whispered. "I am Kim."

It exhausted my eloquence, but they no longer cared. They grabbed me by the hand, pushed each other aside, threw their arms around my neck, kissed me, dragged me to my feet. I had a fleeting thought about my companions in the synagogue. Would I have learned more about God if I had joined them there? And then I heard, as we walked on together about the village, echoing from the whitewashed buildings and the dirt streets, at nightfall in this ancient homeland that did not cherish its girls, "Keem, Keem, Keem, Keem." My name had become an incantation.

I thought of those girls while I stood at my window,

looking down past the village all the way to the Mediterranean—the sea that had carried those of my people who
survived away from their homeland after Bar Kochba, the
great legendary hero, had failed in his uprising against the
Roman legions during the first century of the Christian
Era. I thought about those girls and wondered when I
would see them again, with their dark eyes of old knowledge. I told myself it had been no commonplace event, that
wandering in the dust streets while my companions sat indoors, the women excluded from the service upstairs behind the screen in the synagogue. Initiation, was it?

Through the doorway of a crumbling house I had seen an
old woman, wrapped in a fraying shawl, crouch down to
place cow dung on a fire. She beckoned me in when she
saw me looking, hobbled over on bare feet, drew me inside. The little room was filled with smoke; it smelled of
too many lives and too much poverty. I drew back when
she placed in my hand a cup of mint tea. The little girls,
who had trooped in after me, were watching my face appre-
hensively, afraid I might refuse this hospitality. I wanted to.
There were circles of grease floating in the pale green liq-
uid, the glass was smudged, and I knew, nevertheless, I was
going to drink it. The old lady watched me as I sipped.
Sweet, hot, fresh as the night sky. I had to wonder whether
wine sipped from a ceremonial goblet on Shabbas was any
more holy than this smudged glass offered, from the fullness of poverty, to a stranger.

I held the glass between my hands when I had finished,
bowed my head over it to thank the old woman, pressed
the glass to my chest. That pleased her; she came up close
to me, took me by the elbow, shook me lightly. Then she
began to talk and chatter with the same urgency the little
girls had shown when they began to love me. She pointed
to her heart, to each of her breasts, and then drew me to the

threshold and pointed to the mountains, just then taking on their purple shadow beneath the sky. I strained toward her with my entire attention, but I could not figure out what she was trying to say. Finally she gave up, took me by the shoulders, drew me down, fixed me with a penetrating gaze, released me.

A short time later I caught sight of my companions from the kibbutz winding back toward the truck parked on the outskirts of the village. It was dark by then; the moon was not yet up. The girls came along with me, looking pleased with themselves, very secretive. They wouldn't let me join my companions, a few streets ahead. They pressed close against me, led me on a route of their own so that I arrived at the truck a good while before the others. And then, in twos and threes, they took themselves off, waving good-bye to me. A tall girl remained with me, holding my hand until everyone else had climbed into the truck. Then she pressed my hand against her heart, whispered my name to me in a meaningful way, and said: "You don forghet uz . . ."

I had thought back to the night of Yom Kippur before now. But always I had been involved in my usual conflict, insisting the event had been "more than ordinary, very significant, guided by some nonrational force," while at the same time I hollered with derision. Distracted by this inability to determine "the true nature of the event," I had not paid attention to my desire to return to the village to see the girls again, or to the fantasy set loose in me when I wondered what the old woman had told me. Could she have asked me why that night was more holy than any other? For the first time, at my window looking down over the valley, I asked myself whether the girls had led me to her deliberately.

The answer to these questions did not come to me for many years. When it arrived finally I did not link it to the little girls, the old woman, the mint tea, the waking rapture at the window. But I had decided to write a story about a sect of women that secretly worshipped the Goddess within traditional Judaism and had done so for the thousands of years since the Hebrew conquest of Canaan, handing the tradition down from mother to daughter.

The idea for this novel, *The Flame Bearers*, came to me in 1978, seven years after I left Israel and returned to California. But I no longer doubt that fiery seeds were cast deep into my imagination during that night walk through the small village in the darkening valley. Not a single man had been visible in the streets. For those hours of sunset we walked and wandered in a women's world, making up incantations, finding ceremonial forms and our own sense of the sacred in the dust streets, outside the synagogue.

The Goddess was with us that night, even if the little girls knew nothing of her. She was there when the small fire was kindled from cow droppings by an old crone stooping over the flames. It was she who helped me put the dirty glass of tea to my lips. I had no need to think of her as an objective reality hidden somewhere in the universe keeping an eye on the world as God is said to do. She was fully present long before I learned to name her. Already then, she had risen from the dark soil, to lend a more than ordinary significance to my encounter with the girls. In darkness she had been born to my imagination, in darkness over the next seven years she continued to ask me questions.

I had gone far when I walked away from my companions and went out wandering with the girls. But I continued to fuss about whether one should trust to irrational events and what their true nature might be and whether the girls' coming upon me in the streets was simply coincidence or some other kind of guidance. And if guidance, on what authority? And if authority, from what source? I had glimpsed the possibility of bringing peace between the skeptic and believer who continued to war within me, but that brief glimpse was all I could achieve.

I stayed awake with these thoughts. I woke wrestling with them as if they were a mighty angel that surely would bless me if only I could get the upper hand. And meanwhile I did not go back to the village, although I lived in Israel for many months. I did not go back although I continued to gaze down longingly at it from my window. Within a few months I no longer thought about the old woman and what she had been trying to tell me. Even today I do not know.

But I had touched the hem of the long skirts of the Goddess, there in the streets on the holiest night of the year. I had tasted her in the cup of tea, looked into her eyes, failed to understand her. To figure out what she had told me I would have to unearth the reasons I fought so militantly against my imagination. Why is this night more holy than any other night? To answer that question I would have to go on following the little girls.

Part Two

DESCENT

It is a slow and painful process, this striving after true inner freedom.

—*An Interrupted Life: The Diaries of Etty Hillesum*

I

A day in spring, many years ago. The overgrown garden behind my house. Red wooden table in the sun. I had gone out to clear the ground for planting, but I slumped indifferently on the rickety bench, counting the bricks in the patio.

I had returned from Israel. I had married again. Now I was taking "time out" to examine this feeling that I had become a barren ground. I knew at times this lassitude was part of my larger undertaking. I knew, vaguely, this inertia must have grown out of my efforts to expose my selflessness as a woman. But I could not be more specific than that.

I spent my days indoors. Usually, my husband would get my daughter off to school. At times, I had to force myself to get up, get dressed, eat something, face the day. Frequently I would wander about the house, dusting and straightening. By noon I was lying on my bed in my study (a pompous name for this room where my books were arranged on shelves now rarely disturbed). I had, after years of devotion to books, developed a distrust of reading.

C. G. Jung, a hero of mine several years earlier, had fallen into eclipse. One of the few tasks I accomplished in those days was the rearrangement of my bookshelves. Without any particular plan, I moved *Jung's Collected Works* to the top shelf below the ceiling, where it could only be reached by climbing on the desk. Over the last months, I had begun to see that he was describing the transformation of a mind far different from my own. Musing on his work one day when I was standing at my desk, I found that I disliked the heroism of his night-sea-journey. The hero sets out into the unknown, endures various trials, slays the goddess. Jung interpreted this mythic voyage as a symbolic expression of the individuation process. What the hero endures in these ancient tales, Jung wrote, contemporary people experience within their psyche. We dream the images of transformation that mythic heroes live out in their stories.

Before, I had always identified with this heroic goddess-slayer, transforming himself on his road of trials. But now, staring at my bookshelves, I found myself thinking: Why is he killing her? Why on earth is he killing her? If I had the chance to get that close to her . . . I'd throw myself into her arms.

Would I?

This question did not sit quietly. It located itself in my body and in my mind. I felt it pounding in my temples, beating against my veins, causing a rush of heat and cold that now produced a mental image of a massive, dancing, female figure. I knew at once: the years of initiation had been leading me to this image. "So this is the goddess," I found myself saying as I gazed at her incredulously, her huge breasts lifting and flopping. She picked up her knees, stretched out her arms, bent from the torso in a ponderous dance that was sacred and ridiculous, was taking place at the center of my head, in my sinews and veins, in the room around me and nowhere at all.

Hours must have passed during which I did not move from my desk. Thinking back to them they seem the slowest hours I have ever lived. In them, I visited again the val-

ley of black sheep in the mountains above Dublin. I walked
with the girls through the village below my kibbutz. Wandered by myself in the rose garden in Berkeley, on the
beach in San Francisco, by the reservoir at Mt. Tamalpais.
Seeking something I did not dare to name. The goddess
dancing. It was this fecund image I had been trying to find
in nature, in the dark ground of my self, wherever I
looked, in whatever I read.

The goddess danced and disappeared and grew back into
visibility again. Massive and graceful, she reconciled opposites. She was comforting, dangerous, fearful, inspiring. I
felt that new life would grow from her, that I, myself,
egged on by her image, would soon learn to perform this
heavy, fleet-footed dance of the self. Wherever she stepped,
whatever she touched, quickened and flowered. Her
shadow fell; there was water, before there had been only
rock. She was mother and daughter, ageless and youthful.
She turned her head to gaze at me. I saw the shadow of a
younger woman. Her body was childlike, unformed. She
was kneeling next to a woodland pool. Her left hand covered her eyes. She seemed to be waiting. For me to wake
her? To speak her name? Was it my first image of the
Woman Who Is Not Yet? If so, I did not yet recognize her.
I was in the most extreme state of tranquillity I had ever
experienced, while at the same time I felt that my mind was
moving fast around this still point of urgency where the
goddess was dancing, her daughter kneeling.

I did not turn to look at my books. I knew where they
were, could have reached out with my eyes closed to pluck
down a relevant volume. I sat there going over the shelves
the way I had seen my father play a chess match, blind-
folded. I realized: the books I had loved from the time I
was a girl, reading the classics of Marxism, had concerned
themselves with this dualism, this ceaseless warfare be-

tween opposites, that had been obsessing me since I had fallen on my knees, worshipping a tree. Perhaps this conflict explained why culture did not give a suitable place within itself to the goddess and her daughters?

Nietzsche, in *The Birth of Tragedy*, fascinated by the eternal wrestling match between Dionysus and Apollo, had been studying this self-division. But was Dionysus associated with the goddess?

Dionysus, raised by nymphs on the isle of Naxos; disguised by Ino as a girl; taught by Silenus the secrets of nature . . . yes, this wandering boy of girlish beauty followed by nymphs and maenads had been an initiate into the mysteries of the Goddess Rhea. It was she who dressed him in the fawn skin, dropped a band of vine leaves on his head, sent him out to teach her intoxication. He, trailing his rapture through the vineyards, came up out of the female side of things. His revel and riot were part of it, too; his descent into the underworld to bring his mother Semele up to Olympus; his divine madness, his love of nature, his dissolving of boundaries, his reweaving of the torn web of original Oneness—weren't these the mysteries he learned from Rhea, primal Goddess?

I'd always loved the stories of Dionysus returning to Thebes, his birthplace, in a triumphal procession led by elephants. The Theban women had recognized him, they celebrated him as a God. They followed him up to the mountains to join in his wild revels: danced, dressed in animal skins, immersed themselves in woodland pools. Surely I had always seen myself in them?

And there was Apollo, God of music and the dance, protector of flocks, patron of new towns, serene poet, Lord of the Silver Bow. He had led the Muses from their frenzied dance on Mt. Helicon, persuaded them to join him in his stately measure. Nietzsche had imagined him dreaming an

illusion of freedom from all extravagant urges. This lucent
god of unshakable confidence in his illusions—wasn't he
my lordly principle of reason?

Freud. I had spent hours immersed in his vision of the
individual torn between the instinctual chaos of the id
(with its urges and passions) and the common-sense ego,
riding the id like a man on horseback, reining it in all so
reasonably—wasn't it the same drama written over again?

The Old Testament torn by struggle between the con-
quering "ethical" Hebrews and the natives of Canaan with
their sensual nature worship; Marx's dialectic, derived
from Hegel, thesis and antithesis driving history forward
through the class struggle. Laing's schizoid self, split apart
into self and body. Someday I would have to figure out if
the alienated working class, the chaotic id, the untram-
meled Dionysian ecstasy, the "abominations" of Canaan,
the despised and dissociated body were all lined up on the
female side of things, were ruled, therefore, symbolically
by the goddess.

I got off my desk and began to pace around the room. I
could always become a scholar tomorrow or the next day.
For now, it was enough that I had seen this self-division
branch into culture, move down through the ages, make its
way into political thought, shape history, write itself back
into the origins of consciousness. If I was in conflict between the mother and the father gods, I wasn't the only
one. What I had felt wandering about by myself all those
years was a conflict between thinking and feeling, mind and
body, reason and emotion, that had characterized our culture, perhaps from the start. To resolve this conflict, if such
an idea were even thinkable, one would have to go down to
the origins of things. Down. A descent. Back to the beginnings.

II

A woman is sitting across from me, talking. She has stretched out her arm on the arm of the chair; now she leans toward it. She is speaking about feelings that come to her seldom. She does not know the name for these feelings. She knows that they "suck" at her, pulling her down, "like a vacuum," "tugging" at her. She says if she were not sitting here with me today, she would not be able to tolerate this.

She bends her body from the waist, bends toward her arm on the arm of the chair. Her head drops lower, her dark hair falls forward, covering her face. Her legs rise slowly from the floor, are tucked up next to her, right arm dropping down to enclose them.

She says: "If there were someone in this room who could read body language . . ."

"What would they see?"

"How I keep moving around, how restless I am . . ."

"I think they might see someone curled up like a fetus."

"They would? I am?" She looks over at me. "I am!" she agrees, without moving from the fetal posture. "Did it go back that far?"

I remain silent. To enter into these feelings, she must endure a frightening return to early childhood, its terrifying intensity, uncompromising vehemence, its lost knowledge. If she is not ready for this, I do not want to prompt her. The timing of this descent must be her own.

I wait, aware of the silence. Usually she is a fast talker. Frequently she comes late and says, before she sits down in her chair, "I know, I'm coming late because I don't want to be here." Then, she starts telling me, at top speed, what is going wrong with her life. I listen; soon she will interrupt herself. "I know," she will say, "I'm chattering because I don't want to feel close to you." And finally, discovering it again each time: "I make interpretations to keep you from making them."

Estelle is a woman of cool and formidable intellect. We could spend years throwing interpretations back and forth. That way, we might miss the moment she feels close to me. Fortunately, it is impossible to keep up this talk for fifty minutes. Usually she runs out of things to say. Then she looks at me with a terrified expression. Today, this silence has come early.

"You look frightened," I say.

"Yes, I am frightened," she repeats. Then she falls silent. This is a new voice; its timbre deeper, the voice is childlike, capable of direct and simple statements. She herself looks different, younger and more weary.

Estelle comes here from a day of filming. A successful television personality, she is always well dressed, well made-up. She has interpreted this as another way of evading me. She has never agreed to make an appointment before she goes to work. "Trying to catch me with my face off?" she fences.

I am watching her face. Someone has just rubbed off the mask. For the first time I can see what I have sensed was there—passionate outrage, ravaged exhaustion, desperate need. These flow across her features in visible waves and now she is breathing heavily, has closed her eyes; she is bending over, curling up in a compact ball, her body shaking. She says, her voice soft now, "I'm sinking down into it . . ."

I recognize this moment. I have come to it myself, watched other women enter it. If one can stay with this sensation of being sucked down one will come upon a subterranean world of feeling that has always, before now, eluded one—causing restlessness and sleepless nights, creating pains and tensions in the body, compelling one to reach for a drink, a cigarette, food. Now there will be no need for interpretation.

There is much to be said about the fact that I am in this chair listening while she is in that chair talking. To get here, I have had to pass through the experience she will now enter. If all goes well I will be for her a glimpse into her future. She is my past. My presence will assure her that there indeed is, as she has often wondered, "another side to all this."

Estelle is not familiar with the word *initiation*. She is not aware of an interest in the goddess. Nevertheless, she passed through a crisis many years ago. It can be told briefly.

She married young, before finishing college, moved to suburbia, became a gourmet cook. She spent her time buying clothes, entertaining her husband's friends and employers. Then, one day, inexplicably, she began to grow tired of it all.

In the sixth year of her marriage she "took her life in her own hands." Her husband fell in love with her again, they began jogging together, worked out in a gym. "I had a purpose," she says. "The only trouble was, how long can you give your life meaning through making muscles? One day I sat down on the floor in the gym. I looked at my perfect, rippling thighs. 'Honey,' I said to myself, 'where are you going to go from here?'" It was a cold day in winter; a few days later she got in the car, took her husband to lunch, told him she wanted a divorce.

Here then is the moment of impulse. It had effect. Estelle went back to college, took a degree in media and communications. There, she discovered that she was "fashionably bulimic," a "great talker." She got hired to do an experimental early morning TV show. "Nutrition, Yoga, spatterings of Eastern philosophy, ragtags of feminism, my own yearning for something that would endure, all mixed up in a smooth-talking, easy-flowing hype that disguised my emptiness."

She feels now that she "took a wrong turn, somewhere." That she was headed for something "rich and meaningful" the day she packed her clothes, left the suburban home. "I had just taken a good bite out of my future. 'Lady,' I said to myself, 'you can be anything in the world you want to be.' So tell me, how does it happen this empty shell talking nonstop day and night is what I've become?"

She walked out of the suburban home. She knew she could become anything she wished to be. Nothing happened. It was an impulse, snipped back early, in which a profound self-division made itself known. She was keeping a notebook, in which she recorded dreams and "bits of self-analysis." Recently, looking it over again, she has discovered a conflict between her desire for "fame-success-a-career," and something she regarded as "weird, altogether weird."

What was it? She had wanted to become a painter.

Speaking of it, she smirks, grimaces, makes a disparaging gesture. She throws back her head and laughs. She looks over at me, expecting to find me complicit in this laughter. And at the same time, from some hidden place behind her eyes, showing definite hope I will make some other response. "You're not laughing, huh? Isn't that the richest thing you ever heard?"

"Why not a painter, or anything else you wanted to be?"

"Come on. I'll bet you say that to all the ladies. Me, a painter?"

I wait. This question will have to answer itself. Together, we wait a long time. We live through weeks of "chatter and smoke screen." One day, she says: "You know why I couldn't paint? You know why I rushed back to school and kept myself busy and distracted myself from what was really going on? I thought, If I become a painter everyone will think it's just a pastime. You know? A Sunday watercolor kind of thing. They'd never take me seriously, you know? Here I was, a woman living on alimony, dabbling with paints. I had to go out there and prove myself in their world. And anyway, anyway," she says, faltering, hunching over, glancing at me with a searching gaze, "could I face myself, standing before a canvas every morning? Standing there, facing the emptiness? Facing . . . ?"

She is groping for words, she the smooth talker.

"You know what really happened to me? You want to know? I was sitting with my sketch pad in the park one day. I hadn't drawn a thing since I was a brat with buck teeth and braids. What was I drawing? You want to hear? I was drawing a fat woman. I saw her over there by the garbage cans, digging around. A bag lady, you know? But on the page she was this great big juicy mother. You just wanted to go over and take a big bite out of her. Huge tits, you know? A great huge sagging stomach? One day she was scratching herself and she looked over at me; she put her hands under her tits and thrust out her chest at me. Can you see it? I couldn't stop drawing her. Every day I went back there, she went back there, that was her territory, see? I sketched her in every sort of pose. Bending over, stretching out, holding those mighty knockers of hers. I began to have this weird feeling she was trying to tell me something. Like she had a secret of some kind and I was supposed to figure it out. I'm telling you, I looked at those sketches when I got home one day and I thought, 'Estelle, this is what you're going to do with your life? You're going to sit there like an overgrown infant, drawing boobs?' I crumpled them up and threw them away. But the truth is, I was scared. It's easier to do it their way. Fame-success-a-career, you know? The truth is . . . if I had kept on sketching like that, who knows what would have come out of me?"

Estelle has probably never seen a photograph of the Venus of Willendorf, with her protruding abdomen and pendulous breasts. She has probably never heard of the Neolithic Virgin, holding her hands to her breasts. Nevertheless, disguised as a bag lady, the goddess emerged from this woman who would laugh her head off if I suggested she had, over the years, been involved in an initiation that had drawn her from the conventional side of things. And probably, when she got done laughing, she would have to weep to think that one day she came face to face with the goddess, didn't recognize her, tore her out of her sketch pad, threw her away—and with her, for the time being at least, the possibility of that larger development for which the goddess stands.

The woman who sits in the chair across from me, in fetal position, had reached a conflict. It confronted her with a choice. She took the road more traveled; it was inevitable for one who could only place the goddess with the garbage. Since then, she has been living with a "gnawing sense of desolation" that "hits her in the eyes" the moment she stops running around. It was despair that led her to this chair, where soul-searching takes place, where one is allowed to curl up and go back to the past, to the "brat with buck teeth and braids," who still exists there.

III

Women speak: they describe a time when they "felt frozen," "like stone," when they were "buried in sand." Some feel "inwardly dead." All think back with astonishment to a time when they experimented, changed, came to life, made discoveries. Now they stay in bed, watch soap operas. They drag themselves downstairs to the potting studio, sit bent forward, leaning on their elbows, staring at the wheel. They thumb through old notebooks. They are peering into someone else's life, they say. They neglect children, home, and family, their work and study, not because dreams and intuitions pull them out of their daily routine but because the roots of meaning in their lives have dried up, are withering. They have entered a world of broken images, dry stone, dead trees that give no shelter. Usually, they have no idea that they have come upon a conflict so primitive the whole thing can only be cast in sand. Frozen. Turned to stone. Made inert. Few guess that this wasteland is inevitable for those who have unclothed the paper doll who pretends to be a woman.

Many women are familiar with this struggle; few name it correctly or associate it with an underlying quest to create a self. The vitality and promise of a new enterprise come to an end. Few connect this spectacular deflation to a conflict that has been running along beneath the surface, doggedly pursuing. We may have managed, for a time, to silence it by the rapture and enthusiasm of the work to which we have committed ourselves, as it seems, wholeheartedly. But the heart of women is not yet whole. It is profoundly divided. In women, this great duality we have observed in Freud and Nietzsche and Laing is experienced as a struggle between inner and outer self. It finds expression when women write diaries.

"Two Nellys live in me," writes Nelly Ptaschkina, a fifteen-year-old Russian girl who kept a diary. "Sometimes I would like to know which is the real one. When I am in that other world 'that' Nelly seems the real one; when I am back again in my ordinary, every day one it is 'this.' In fact they complete each other and make up the real me."

Anne Frank had a similar concept of the self. "He's a darling," she wrote of her boyfriend Peter, "but I soon closed up my *inner self* from him. If he wants to force the lock again he'll have to work a good deal harder than before."

Emily Carr: "I used to write diaries when I was young but if I put anything down that was *under the skin* I was in terror that someone would read it and ridicule me, so I always burnt them up before long . . . I wonder why we are always ashamed of our *best parts* and try to hide them."

For Anaïs Nin the diary is the only place a woman can become real. "Playing so many roles, dutiful daughter, devoted sister, mistress, protector, my father's new found illusion, Henry's needed, all-purpose friend, I had to find one place of truth, one dialogue without falsity. This is the role of the diary."

The same theme appears in May Sarton. "I am here alone for the first time in weeks, to take up my 'real' life again at last. That is what is strange—that friends, even passionate love, are not my real life . . ."

Ruth Benedict, in her characteristic way, expresses all the

urgency and turbulence of this problem: "What was my character anyway? My real ME was a creature I dared not look upon—it was terrorized by loneliness, frozen by a sense of futility, obsessed by a longing to stop. No one had ever heard of that Me. If they had, they would have thought it was an interesting pose. The mask was tightly adjusted."

A creature we dare not look up, terrorized by loneliness, obsessed by a longing to stop—this is the creature we must confront before we can establish a true ground of female being. When we wander about near woodland pools it is this frozen self of the interior who moves toward life. But we, who fear this quickening movement, disguise the deep conflict aroused when this banished inner being asks to live.

How do we move from the rock to the pool in the rock? How do we proceed from the wasteland to what lies buried beneath it? How does an individual woman get beyond the paralysis of this conflict she cannot resolve, down to the roots of it, in her childhood?

The woman sitting across from me has not moved for ten minutes. This span of time seems highly significant to us. For her, it is the longest time she has been silent, in this room, with me. Later, reflecting on it, she will say: "Who knows? Maybe it's the longest I've ever been silent since I learned how to talk?"

For Estelle, who has been running from a sense of meaninglessness, it is important to know that in this deadness there is something alive, waiting to be born. She will know this if I know and believe it, even if I do not speak.

She lifts her head to cast a searching gaze at me. I have a sense of opening myself in response to her. I must let her see what is there. Something is happening between us; it tests everything we have achieved so far. I can feel the power of her penetration, searching a place in me usually hidden, guarded over, shut away from another's eyes. She hunches her shoulders and carries on this silent looking. Her face remains solemn, frightened, rapt, anguished. She blinks three times. An electric shock has passed between us. Perhaps now she knows that I, too, have passed through the experience she will undergo, that one day, she, too, will hear grass singing where there was only rock.

Estelle has come out of her fetal position. She is sitting upright, her knees hugged against her chest, her chin pressed down on her knees. Descent is a dropping down into the self. When it is a successful process, endured to the end, it brings a woman into direct contact with events from her childhood so highly charged with conflict they were isolated from consciousness, split off from an active role in her emotional life. If she can tolerate this she will discover that there exists within herself, at the heart of her self-division, a desolate child whom she abandoned early in its development. Who now, if allowed to do so, will provide a starting place from which to build an authentic self.

There are many ways to encounter that child isolated within the self. Often this child appears in dreams, sometimes in a drawing or a doodle; occasionally she is there in the way a woman dresses or one day, suddenly, wears her hair in braids. But the advent of this child cannot fulfill its promise until she is translated from the symbolic to the emotional sphere. When she is encountered during the descent she is an emotional reality, our first conscious awareness that there is a great deal more to us than we have permitted ourselves to know. If we can tolerate this child she will tell us why we have isolated her from participation in our lives—losing with her the roots of female being.

Descent returns one to the past. It is a form of time travel within the self. If it were easy to go back one would not need to cover a fertile conflict with the dryness of the wasteland. To break through that inert rubble a powerful eruption is required.

Estelle has tolerated this sensation today after many weeks of circling around it—feeling it for a second or two and then tearing away from it into her desperate chatter. She has told me she wants to leap out of the chair and race down to the doughnut shop at the bottom of the hill.

Other women say they want to stand up and scream. I hear this often. I remember: an older woman. She had one of those lean, intense, dramatic faces. One day I noticed that the face was behaving the way a face does before it begins to cry—the nose jutting out, cheeks sinking in, pale lips outlined with their own urgency. It is the moment of shock before feeling comes; and then, eyes filling with tears, the heartbreak.

"Why are you crying, can you tell me?"

"For a minute there I thought I was going to scream and scream and scream."

"What stopped you?"

"I noticed . . . you were here."

"The scream comes out of feeling completely alone?"

"Alone with something unspeakably terrible."

" 'Something unspeakably terrible' . . ." I am trying to make the words part of myself, to extract their implication.

"A feeling . . . I'm not sure you'll understand this. A feeling of being sucked down . . ."

"And the tears?"

"The tears were my relief that if it's going to happen, you'll stay with me. My tears were . . . this is a contradiction. They were a feeling like my heart was breaking because the last time . . . the last time this happened . . . there was no one there at all."

"The last time this happened?"

"Did I say that? It's strange . . . I don't think this has ever happened before at all."

"A feeling of being sucked down . . . ?"

"Sucked down . . . descending into a deep pit . . ."

This descent may take place in a single session and not be repeated again for many weeks. It may take place repeatedly, week after week. Some women live for years with a sense that they are being drawn down into themselves, to uncover lost and buried contents.

"I'm being sucked down, I'm dropping down into a deep pit. It's a place of doom and despair. Everything awful is there. Garbage . . . it's filled with garbage. There are high walls. I can't get out. There's no way out. Everything in here is like that so there's no escape."

Her voice has changed while she describes this descent; it has a simplicity and directness I associate with childhood. I ask her:

"How old are you?"

She says without hesitating: "Four or five years old."

"Does light reach there?"

"Yes," she says, looking around her, "yes, it reaches."

"Do you call for help?"

"No one would come."

"You're in this terrible pit and you've completely despaired of getting help in this place?"

"Yes. But the light coming down does seem hopeful . . ."

"No way out?"

"A crane of some sort might come to scoop out the garbage and save me . . ."

"So, you will be saved by whatever comes to get the garbage?"

Another woman; she feels that she has fallen into a sewer. She is looking down at filthy water that makes her gag. She says she is a child, two or three years old. She is alone;

there is no point calling for help. Then she notices a way out . . . a possibility. She sees a rope ladder stretching up to a grid.

The imagery is consistent. A movement inward and down —a sense of being drawn into a whirlpool. There is a place—pit, sewer, cellar, sand pit, dark hole—shut off in exile from other places. There is in this place a lost child in despair.

This desolate child lives in all of us, part of the self we have not yet dared know, essential to encounter if we are to get on with this task of creating an authentic woman. Split off there, in the darkness of unknowing, this child in torment is the reason our development tears itself apart in irresolvable conflict, enters the wasteland, smothers in arid sand the enterprise of becoming a woman. If we are divided against ourselves, it is because we cannot tolerate the suffering of this tormented child we perceive as outcast of the sewer, citizen of the garbage dump—the inevitable imagery for what we have come to fear and despise in the self.

Harry Guntrip, psychotherapist and psychoanalytic theorist, has written cogently of this split self: "If the outer defenses of the cold, unemotional intellectual are penetrated, he reveals a secret, vulnerable, very needy, fear-ridden infantile self, showing up in his dream and fantasy world, though *split off* from the surface self, the false self that the outer world sees."

This part of the self that has been split off is a "part of the infantile ego in which the infant found his world so intolerable that the sensitive heart of him fled into himself."

This part of the self that has been lost is "entirely cut off from all communication with the outer world . . . shut in in an ultimate way." It is a "lost core of the personality"; one cannot "feel or get in mental touch" with it.

One of Guntrip's patients dreamed that she had opened a

locked steel drawer and "inside was a naked baby with wide open expressionless eyes staring at nothing."

Guntrip regards this dream as the "perfect description" of the split self. There is a place apart—a locked steel drawer; there is a living child within it. But its eyes are expressionless. It stares into a desolate void. Guntrip believes that "in some minor degree at least" this split in the self is "practically universal."

A lost core of personality, closed off in an ultimate way, desolate.

It may be that in most of us this child of the self, banished from our experience, is less desperately terrified than was the schizoid baby with expressionless eyes in the locked drawer.

It may be that our courage to endure this descent is buoyed up by a new and radical sense of what it means to be a woman. By an intuition: along with the fear and anguish of the child enclosed in the dark pit there is its potency and vitality of being, its memory of early childhood, its knowledge of the primal mother, that big-bodied, ripe-breasted, awesome one who was our first experience of the mother goddess.

When we draw the curtain over that fearful place of isolation, and abandon the child we were to its lonely shadow life, we lose the guide who might lead us back to this original knowledge of female power.

This is a paradox we must endure. The despised and dependent creature whom we strive to keep buried within ourselves can take us back far more directly than archetypal image or volumes of research to the arms of the Great Mother. This desolate child who constitutes our most potent motive for self-division is our most reliable guide to the powerful goddess.

Descent proceeds by way of paradox. The movement

forward, toward the Woman Who Is Not Yet, rests upon a movement backward into the childhood history of the self. The wasteland proves to be a ground of fertile conflict. The suffering of the divided self uncovers a complete, if desolate, child. That abandoned creature, howling in darkness, holds within itself a knowledge of the Great Mother—she who offers such abundant promise to a woman in quest for a self.

IV

Winter. The sky folded in careful pleats. A cat walks at our feet, rubs against my mother's leg, moves on, selects my daughter. She is nine years old. I have been carrying her jacket over my arm. Now, instead of handing it to her, I put it on. She is little, the jacket is too small for me. I become a child; crouch down, hunch over, begin to clown, tug at the sleeves. "Who's that?" my mother says. My daughter throws her arms around this new companion.

"Zelda," I answer. "This is Zelda."

Zelda was destined to become an important figure in our lives. She was an act I put on, a character I assumed. But she was also something else: more spontaneous, more separate. When she wanted attention she asked for it. When she was angry or jealous she let everyone know. She could burst out in tears, laugh, pout, or express undying devotion. She had spontaneity, candor, immediacy, presence. She had arrived with her own story.

She claimed to be eight years old, said she had spent many years in a cellar room. It was dark there but she could see out a high window. She had limited speech, but an impressive repertoire of grunts and sighs. Later, she would show a native gift for her own id-language.

Zelda is always up to things she should not be doing. She doesn't like to share her food. She carries all the shadows usually shut away in darkness. She is greedy, eats too much, states with pleasure that she is "damn fat." She hates to take baths, will not comb her hair.

I soon figured out that Zelda had come as my guide. This lonely exile, dweller in the ghettos of the self, the very epitome of "the other," had arrived with an undeniable charm. Her candor, the forbidden truths she managed to speak, gave her a whimsical appeal. If I saw my daughter and husband playing together while I was sitting by myself, Zelda would immediately fly off in a storm of envy.

"Zelda's mad," she'd call out to them in her irresistible clown voice, "nobody likes Zelda. She hates people who are having fun. She's lonely. She's gonna make trouble, you'll see."

I would have died rather than admit it on my own behalf. But that is how I was feeling, alone in my study, preoccupied with my gloomy introspection. My daughter, who used to worry about me, was delighted with Zelda. She developed a character of her own, a girl called Miriam, far less intelligent than my brilliant child, more outspoken, much less well behaved. Then a guy named Boris showed up. He was goofy and simple, but was able to support the family by singing in a rock group.

These creatures made room for themselves; they brought to the surface silent tensions that otherwise might have disrupted the family. They bickered, reproached, blamed, and forgave each other. We played together, two adults and a child. We had much in common. All of us had given up feelings now restored to us by these odd clowns.

By hanging out with Zelda over the years I began to see how consistently I, Kim, evaded the emotional truth of any situation. If someone hurt my feelings I smiled and assured him that whatever he had done was just fine. If someone made me angry, I swallowed the rage until it burst out, uncontrollably. If someone frightened me, I acted stoical, indifferent, supremely cool. I had done this all my life without knowing how much of myself I gave away. Now, with Zelda, things were different.

Zelda began to reveal feelings that reached, in their primal vehemence, back to infancy. Zelda, lovable clown, was often in deep anguish. Tears I could not weep, a soul-suffering disguised by eating, a sense of being torn apart at some deep, sensitive core of myself—these inconceivable feelings now returned through Zelda.

The change from happy to sad clown took place over many years, during which Zelda became a regular part of our family. Then she gradually began to appear when I woke after midnight and went out walking through the dark neighborhood. Zelda, who came along, occasionally said surprising things. "Zelda's sad," she'd whisper, "she don't wanna live . . ."

During that time I began to take Zelda very seriously. She was restoring feelings I had driven away because I could not tolerate their intensity, their early despair. A small child in me was sad to the point of suicidal urgency. Only through Zelda could I hear her pain. When I asked Zelda how old she was now she would insist that she was eight years old; then admit, reluctantly, that she was younger. "Zelda's three," she'd say. "Zelda's one years olden. Zelda's a wet brat, Zelda's wearin' stinky diapers." Then Zelda would fall back into a state of feeling so densely primitive it took my breath away.

I had realized, by then, that my "work" during those years consisted of my efforts to get closer to Zelda. She had become the most fruitful endeavor of my life. To acknowledge as mine those primitive feelings she embodied— wasn't that my homegrown version of the struggle that also takes place in psychoanalysis?

When living in Dublin, I had once walked past a mental

hospital. From the upper floor I heard a screech of pain. At first I thought it an inhuman cry. But then I realized: if I called this cry inhuman it was because the anguish and torment it expressed reached beyond my own experience.

I walked on. There was an immense shrouded sun. The cry came after me, expanding my sense of human suffering. It lasted long after I had reached home, miles from the brick hospital on the hill. Sometimes, years later, I heard it again, piercing, heartrending. One day I realized that Zelda was uttering this unthinkable anguish. This cry I had thought inhuman.

Usually, when Zelda was in this state, I went into my study, lay down on the couch, put my head in my arms, waited it out. But one morning Zelda's anguish terrified me. What would come of this experiment? Would I end up in a locked ward in the upper story of a brick building screaming behind barred windows?

I couldn't stand it any longer. I went out of the house fast, got into my car, drove off, turning corners, driving higher, up into the hills.

I parked the car, got out, looked around. I recognized the place; I had been there before. It was a section of Tilden Park that grew wild. Zelda would not be observed. I walked down the dirt path, pushed open the gate, started to run.

I wanted to get away from the parking lot. Something was about to break loose. I had been trying for most of my life to control it. Zelda, child of myself, had dissolved into me. I was throwing myself on the ground. Now I was crying in a hoarse voice. It wasn't Zelda's, it was my own. "Take me back, I can't stand it, take me back . . ."

Eventually I got to my feet. Everything was casting shadows—the eucalyptus trees, their peeling bark, the dried thorn plants next to the path. A bird went by overhead with a sharp cry, drawing its shadow over my shadow. I kept glancing around. Had anyone seen me? I felt ridiculous, exposed. What had I meant by it? Take me back, I can't stand it, take me back . . . ?

There was Zelda again. In high spirits suddenly, she skipped and clapped her hands; she was romping through the fields saying hello to the flowers. Zelda was about to figure out what the old woman who had given me tea in the little village had been trying to tell me.

Zelda said, when the wind blew, it was her own wildness blowing in/there/out/there in the world of herself. She refused to distinguish between inner and outer, gathered up yellow leaves for a bed, wept as she lay down. Some part of her, too, was dying. Zelda took the goddess for granted. She made up names for her, spoke to her irreverently. She called her Big One, Fat Mama, reproached her for letting the leaves die. She called her Hunger Mother, Fat Milk Cushion. Zelda was locked into the world as a young child is locked into the mother, in an ecstatic kinship, the source of original meaning.

I saw: it was no light matter to have lost this response to nature. That loss stood for a far more general loss of relatedness to self and world and all its creatures, an experience for which Zelda taught me to weep and rage when we could not get back into that kinship with the natural world, our first world, our mother-world.

I sat down on a fallen tree. I took out my notebook. Finally I was going to answer the questions that had troubled me since I left Israel. Finally, I was going to reason it all out.

The desolation hidden away in the female psyche, our inability to build an authentic female self, arose from the loss of relationship to the mother-world of early childhood. That, too, is a world in which subject and object have

not yet been separated. It is a time before child-body and
mother-body have been wrenched apart into two separate
bodies, child and mother sharing a mouth-breast, a tongue-
nipple, child not other than what it sees: breast, hand, tree,
shadow, light, all part of the mother part of the self . . .

If life seemed abundant then, teeming and luxurious, at
the breast of the mother, tropical paradise where food arose
magically out of that mountainous flesh of her, it is no
wonder all subsequent sense of nature will be mixed in with
our first impression of the mother. It lasts a long time, this
merged world of earliest being. The periods of consciousness slowly growing, the sensations threading themselves
together, becoming fixed and permanent impressions. So
that the hand we look upon remains a hand and does not
dissolve again into the light that surrounds it or become a
head moving toward us or a breast toward which we are
ourselves moving. But even then, looking up from her
arms, we think she has drawn a blue sky behind her head or
a tree to look over her shoulder. Falling asleep on her breast
we know her as our mountain of repose. Waking, we see
she has lifted her hand; we gaze into the cave at the pit of
her arm and we turn, settling ourselves more deeply into
her valleys.

She, awesome one, primal mother. Earth of us mother,
our feeding and touching and feeling and first seeing and
sensing, our reaching out and finding and all our knowing
spun round the softness and fullness and abundance of the
woman-body of the mother of all.

Of course, how could I have missed it before? Naturally,
to the infant the primal mother is the goddess. The original
earth mother. Mother Nature. The Great Mother from
whom all things emerge.

Whatever else the goddess may also be in the universe,
whatever kind of power working through nature, presiding

over the world, we know her first as the human mother just as we first knew that mother as woman complete in herself, awesome in her capacities, all-knowing, dreadful and compassionate, not yet divided, intrinsically whole. The Great Goddess, whether as psychic image or external reality, will always be far more than the human mother could ever be. But the human mother, as we first know her in infancy, will always be for her child a goddess.

This then was what we longed for when we went out into nature—this original knowledge of woman in her power, which we have locked away with that desolate child who knew the primal mother and whose anguish over the loss of her has caused us to cast the child out of ourselves. If we cannot tolerate the desolation of this loss we cannot regain our original knowledge of female power. Our future as women is built upon this paradox and our capacity to resolve it.

When a woman, divided within herself, seeks for wholeness and authentic power, does not know where to look for them, goes forward, hesitates, the mother goddess speaks. From dreams, from nature, from memory, she leads our development forward by guiding us into the past, to a reexperience of the time we knew the mother in her majesty, before we split off this knowledge, losing with it the fundamental roots of female being.

What does it take to get back to the roots? What keeps us from unearthing their power?

With these questions I found myself at the bottom of the descent. There I was, knocking with small fists at the gates to the underworld. I shut my notebook, closed my eyes. The dark-eyed girls ran toward me on the dust streets, shouting and pointing. The old woman brought me a cup of tea. This time there was no hesitation.

Zelda grabbed it.

Part Three

UNDERWORLD

From the "great above" she set her
  mind toward the "great below,"
The Goddess, from the "great
  above" she set her mind toward
  the "great below,"
Inanna, from the "great above"
  she set her mind toward the
  "great below."

My lady abandoned heaven,
  abandoned earth,
  To the nether world she
  descended,
Inanna abandoned heaven,
  abandoned earth,
  To the nether world she
  descended
Abandoned lordship, abandoned
  ladyship,
  To the nether world she
  descended.

—SUMERIAN MYTH

I

In Christian mythology no one wants to go to the underworld. Sinners are sent down there after death to receive retribution from fire that is everlasting and unquenchable. In the underworld the archfiend lay chained on the burning lake of hell, a place of outer darkness, perpetual torment.

In Greek mythology people keep going down to the underworld before they are dead. Hermes, a god, goes down and comes back constantly. But the souls of the dead he guides into Hades never return.

Persephone went down into the underworld because she was abducted by Hades: torn out of her mother's arms, torn away from the maidens with whom she was playing. Then, because she ate the seven seeds of the pomegranate, she got stuck there and could only go back to visit Demeter, her mother, during the spring.

According to this tale, Persephone had no choice about going or staying.

There is a hungry dog standing guard at the entrance to the underworld. Heracles figured out the way to kidnap him, leaving the path to the underworld open. He wrestled with Cerberus. The sweat from his brow bleached the leaves of the poplar wreath he wore. A mighty labor, wrestling with hunger.

Theseus, the Athenian hero, slayer of the Minotaur, destroyer of Goddess worship in Crete, went down to Hades to reabduct Persephone. He was bound fast in the Chair of Forgetfulness. We are grateful to Theseus for reminding us. It is possible to forget in the underworld. We, however, are going down there to remember.

Orpheus went down to Hades to find his lost love but lost her again when he was almost out of there. Lacking faith, he turned around too soon. He was trying to make sure he really had her by the hand. He needed the reassurance of his eyes; he couldn't trust to his other senses. We will walk straight ahead, looking neither to right or to left. We will trust our senses.

The underworld: hard to drop into it when you choose to go. Hard to gain entrance if you haven't yet wrestled with hunger. Hard to remember what you are there for once you arrive. Nearly impossible to get out leading your love by the hand. That is what these old stories tell us. If we're lucky, persuasive enough, good enough at remembering, the odds are good that we shall find our long-lost love again.

Yes, the odds are good. Better than might be apparent. Even the Christian underworld took its name from a goddess. From Hel, Norse Queen of the Dead. Her "hell" had little in common with our hell. People did not go down there to be punished. They did not go down there for muscular exploits. In the Goddess-underworld there is no retribution or outer darkness. Hel's hell was a uterine shrine, a sacred cave of rebirth.

Shamans of the far north believed they could put on a Hel-met, become invisible, go down into the underworld without dying, come back to earth transformed. That precisely is what we, too, are going to do.

The same kind of story is told in the Pacific. There Mother Death is thought to be a fire-mountain. You go to her by passing through a sacred cave.

Pele, the Hawaiian volcano goddess, bathed the souls of the dead in regenerating fire.

Japan's sacred volcano was named for the fire goddess Fuji: "Grandmother, Ancestress."

In Malekula, there is an old song full of hope and optimism. "Abiding in the fire is bliss," sing the dead ruled by the Goddess. "There is no fear of being consumed."

That is a hell one wouldn't mind getting into. An underworld where the Goddess rules over our rebirth. Where fire is regenerative. Where pomegranates grow wild.

There are stories about Persephone that say she was in the underworld because it was always her kingdom. She didn't have to be raped and carried away into it by an intrusive god. She ruled it as death goddess from the start. And therefore, when she wanted to leave, she left.

The furniture of the underworld: lakes, worms, pomegranates, chairs of forgetting, purgative fires, ovens and bread. Ovens and bread? Infernus, the hell of classical paganism, took its name from *fornix*, an earth-oven. Ancient Roman saying: "The oven is the mother." "So, you got a loaf baking in the oven?" my grandmother used to say when one of her daughters was pregnant.

There were also Ladies of Bread—harlot-priestesses of the Goddess temples, closely associated with ovens and bakeries. These ladies were given to orgies, which went by the name *fornacalia*, which means oven-feasts. From this word we get two familiar words of our own. *Furnace.* And *fornicate.* Apparently, in Infernus one gets fed by bread baked in the oven-mother.

That's good, because we are now going into the house of Hel in search of the mother who once was our goddess, and who fed us.

II

I began to interest myself in the underworld when I fell into it and could not get out. Dreaming, I had walked down a spiral staircase that opened from under my desk into an earth room on a lower floor of my house. I found it a fascinating place and was happy to be there, playing with a fountain that would suddenly turn into a stream of fire when I held out my hands to it. But then I noticed that the spiral staircase had disappeared. I was shut in there; I couldn't get out again. I had been locked up in the underworld.

This dream proved to be prophetic. I spent the next several years closed into myself. I had separated from my second husband by then. My daughter had gone off to college. There was nothing to call me back out of this Hel-ish place into which I had dropped. I rarely went out of the house; days passed during which I scarcely left my study. I had a small bed in there and frequently, having dressed and come downstairs to work, I wrapped myself in a heavy blanket, lay down on my bed, fell into a waking dream.

A drawbridge was lowered from a castle. Knights and ladies rode across it; I went with them and was led, fully awake, into a dank room below the earth. The door to the dungeon clanged shut behind me. I found myself kneeling before a vague, female shape suspended between floor and ceiling. It was both blissful and exciting to have come down here and was at the same time a formidable anguish.

This quality of holding polar opposites together proved to be characteristic of the underworld. In my dream the fountain had bubbled fire and water. In my reverie I was in a painful state of bliss, suspended between waking and sleeping, as if I had dropped into an archaic consciousness familiar perhaps to a very small infant. It was an imagistic consciousness, around which external reality seemed to float, present but not attended to, while I drifted in a sea of half awareness, bathed in half impressions, vivid imagery, and strong bodily sensations, all of them presided over by hovering female shapes or fragments.

Waking from this state it seemed to me that I had managed to make my way back into the lived-memory of the first hours of my life. There I was again, infant swimming in and out of a womb-state of preconscious existence, inner and outer not torn apart yet one from the other; who she was and I not yet distinguished; the breast around which my hand closed not different from my hand closing. It was this primal state of mind that had broken through in the first rapturous responses I had made to nature. It was this undivided condition Zelda held within herself and brought back to me, a consciousness where the individual was still embedded in the universe with a vivid and meaningful sense of participation based upon powerful feelings and strong sensual responses. This was the Goddess world, known first in the arms and at the breast of the primal mother.

When I would awaken from my Hel-ish reveries I sometimes felt drained and exhausted. But always, within a few hours, I would find that my effort to understand what I had experienced "down there" in the infernal regions of myself had pushed my thought past all the barriers that formerly confined it. I filled notebooks with diagrams and notes and speculations about the origin of the ego, the possibility of descending into earlier, archaic states of consciousness, the role of anxiety and the superego in warding off this return. I could easily imagine that creativity and religious feeling both were derived from this archaic, primal consciousness of the young infant adrift in its mother's arms, and it seemed to me a great pity that until now I had known so little about this entire primordial realm. For in this archaic consciousness of the infant there resided the fullest possible memory of the primal mother as goddess. There, in that dark and murky realm of first impressions, was the seed bed of women's original power.

But why had it all been lost? Why had this first, rapturous sense of participation in the mother-world been lost? Why had we found it necessary to split off this memory of first bliss and of original oneness with female power?

Living in the underworld: one falls down into questions, kicks, tosses about, wails a bit, knows some bliss, and re-emerges with a splinter of possibility that could be taken for an answer. And there are books, too, in the underworld, standing helter-skelter on the rough shelves cut into the earth. Fully waking one day from my waking-dream I remembered that Freud had speculated, in *Civilization and Its Discontents,* about this same "oceanic consciousness" with which I was preoccupied. Why not see what Freud had to say about it?

The phrase "oceanic consciousness," as I recalled, came from Romain Rolland, who had written to Freud in response to *The Future of an Illusion,* in which Freud had discussed the illusory nature of religious belief. Rolland, who shared his judgment about religion, suggested that Freud had, nevertheless, overlooked the basic ground of religious sentiment, in a feeling that he called "a sensation of 'eternity,' a feeling as of something limitless, unbounded—as it were 'oceanic.'" According to Rolland, this feeling was not an article of faith, but a strong, subjective impression, bringing with it no guarantees of personal immortality. A person capable of experiencing this feeling, Rolland said, might rightly regard himself as religious, without subscribing to any other article of belief.

Freud, pursuing this idea in *Civilization and Its Discontents*, admitted that he was entirely unable to discover this "oceanic" feeling in himself. Nevertheless, he speculated about its meaning and origins and came to think of it as a sense of an "indissoluble bond, of being one with the external world as a whole." Freud then went on to derive this "oceanic" feeling from the state of consciousness possessed by the infant at the breast—when it does not as yet "distinguish its ego from the external world as the source of the sensations flowing in upon him." With the help of Rolland, Freud had tentatively located the *"fons et origo* of the whole need for religion" in a state of infantile consciousness first experienced at the mother's breast.

I was interested in these ideas. They were a reassuring confirmation of my own oceanic experiences in the underworld. I took the book down from its shelf, curled up with it in my heavy blanket, and began to read. If Freud associated this primordial consciousness with the mother, perhaps he could tell me something about the way it had been lost?

To begin with I was not disappointed. Freud went on to inquire whether we have "a right to assume the survival of something that was originally there, alongside of what was later derived from it." I hoped he would answer this question affirmatively, since my experience in the underworld seemed definitely to be telling me that a primordial state of consciousness had survived alongside the later ego-consciousness derived from it. And in fact, Freud answered this question unambiguously. "Undoubtedly," he said. ". . . In the realm of the mind . . . what is primitive is so commonly preserved alongside of the transformed version which has arisen from it that it is unnecessary to give instances as evidence."

That was reassuring, since my own sojourn in the house of Hel was daily proving to me that it was possible to actively reexperience this archaic consciousness to which the ego is usually denied access. But, how was it possible? Freud asked himself this question too and then accounted for the simultaneous presence, within the mind, of the primitive and the more evolved, with reference to a divergence in development. One portion of an "attitude or instinctual impulse" remains unchanged, while another portion undergoes further development. He concluded this particular discussion with the following observation: ". . . in mental life nothing which has once been formed can perish . . . everything is somehow preserved and . . . in suitable circumstances (when, for instance, regression goes back far enough) it can once more be brought to light."

I had already come to suspect that what Freud called regression—a retreat from a more advanced to an earlier stage of development because of fear—I would myself regard as part of a heroic quest for self-knowledge. But psychoanalysts in general seemed very clear about the nature of regression. "A person who has been hurt by the world may shut himself up in a private dream world. Moral anxiety may cause a person to do something impulsive so that he will be punished as he was when he was a child. Any flight from controlled and realistic thinking constitutes a regression."

Was I involved in a flight from "controlled and realistic thinking"? Was I living in my own private dream world?

Had I retreated to it in fear of the developmental process in which I was involved? Or did my sojourn in the underworld, this prolonged period in which I was, admittedly, cut off from friends and acquaintances, constitute a valid movement forward into the next stages of female development, in which the oceanic, archaic mother-consciousness would be called back from its primitive infantile state, invited to undergo development, and then be reunited with the later ego-consciousness that had originally evolved from it? Wasn't that, in fact, the very process in which I had been involved during the last decades of my life?

I returned to Freud. Did he have something to say that would clarify the nature of this peculiar dream state in which I was plunged, and help me perhaps connect its loss to the loss of the early mother? He had begun promisingly, I felt, by associating the oceanic feeling with the unboundedness of the first relationship between mother and child, the infant's sense of an unbounded relationship to the universe, its merged sense of identity with the mother's breast. Where would he go from here, then?

"Thus we are perfectly willing to acknowledge that the 'oceanic' feeling exists in many people, and we are inclined to trace it back to an early phase of ego-feeling. The further question then arises, what claim this feeling has to be regarded as the source of religious needs."

This was of course the urgent question for me, too. If the oceanic feeling of primordial consciousness at the mother's breast was the source of religion it would clearly be the source of a Goddess religion and worship that took as its central motif the mother, the female body, mother nature, the Mother Goddess. This oceanic consciousness, with its inherent knowledge of female power, might well be the fundamental and until now missing ground of our new female identity. Breathlessly then I turned the pages of his little book to see what Freud would make of this question. Alas, having come this far, Freud dismisses Rolland's claim without further ado as not highly compelling. No, he says: in and of itself this oceanic consciousness (associated with the mother and her breast) could not be the source of religious feeling. Moving quickly now, he points out that a feeling can only be a "source of energy" if it is derived from a strong need. Well, I could agree with that, too. I had been tracking a feeling dating back to the mother's arms, unbounded and oceanic in nature, possibly at the heart of all religious striving. It would seem evident then that the psychological need derived from the oceanic feeling would be a need to be reunited with the mother, original source of relatedness and bliss. That seemed to match up very well with my own speculations and experience. But this was not the conclusion to which Freud was suddenly leaping. Far from it. I now saw that he had, within the scope of a single paragraph, sharply veered off from infantile helplessness and longing that might be associated with the mother, and conjured up the father instead, thus locating religious feeling in the child's need for patriarchal protection. "I cannot think," he writes, "of any need in childhood as strong as the need for a father's protection." What? I thought, sitting up on my underworld bed, throwing back my covers. Freud cannot imagine any need as strong as the need for a father's protection? He's admitting that? He cannot imagine the earliest, infantile need to be protected by the mother? To be at one with her? To be nurtured by her? To be made part of her power?

So there I was, adrift in my oceanic state, which Freud, by his own admission, could not discover in himself. But I had already begun to suspect that Freud would always substitute a father for a mother when he was thinking about childhood. And therefore I was not surprised when Freud now went on to confess that, where such states of mind were concerned, it was "very difficult for me to work with these almost intangible quantities."

What a pity, however, that Freud could not push himself further on this point. He was right at the edge of discovering the significant association between the child's first relationship to the mother, and its subsequent experience of those altered states of consciousness that have become so fascinating to our time. Recognizing his limits here, he calls up yet another friend to make the association between "primordial states of mind" and Yoga, mysticism, ecstasy, and trances. But alas, this association, which seemed so fascinating to me (because of the possibility that meditative states of mind, mysticism, and ecstasy are natural to women), Freud himself felt reluctant to pursue. Taking refuge in the words of Schiller's diver, Freud prematurely closed this promising section of his famous work with the following quotation:

> . . . Es freue sich,
> Wer da atmet im rosigten Licht.

> Let him rejoice
> Who breathes up here in the roseate light!

Exit Freud from the underworld, where he might have discovered the fascinating relationship between natural creativity, religion, ecstasy, mysticism, inherent female power, the Great Goddess, and the mother.

III

I have known other women who spent a season in the underworld. All of them talk about it in the same way. It kept them indoors most of the time, wrapped up in blankets or quilts, in some dark corner of a room they trusted. A surprising number of them have gone up and down, in dreams and waking visions, upon a spiral staircase. They have sipped from fountains that turn to fire; scalded themselves on fresh water breaking upward from the earth. The underworld: earth and fire, water and roots. The sense that one is being nourished by the oceanic state of consciousness itself, being fed by the roots of things, by what is fundamental.

In the underworld a woman enters a state of mind far more active than memory. She unearths the actual experience of reaching out, discovering fingers, learning how to grasp, taking hold with a hand that is three days old. In the underworld a woman grasps for the first time the breast of the mother goddess.

In the beginning, when I first went down to live in the underworld, I didn't know how to behave like Hermes, coming and going at will. I felt the way Persephone must have, in those stories in which she's been abducted and can't go back. But then the drawbridge would go down, the spiral staircase would disclose itself, I would be wandering up or wandering down, pursuing always the same urgent question.

One day, in this state of sleepy wakefulness, I saw myself shaped like a question mark as I made my way down the spiral stairs. I burst into laughter. It was true: all other life had faded away, leaving me face to face with my still un-answered question.

One goes down into the underworld to ask why. Why had this archaic consciousness of early childhood been split off from the ego's development, so that human beings raised in a patriarchal culture came to have highly devel-oped "realistic" minds but not highly evolved "oceanic" minds? Why should the ego have developed its linear capac-ities at the expense of its associative possibilities?

I went over the ground I had covered so far. On the one hand, here was the infant born into the mother-world, often in a state of such helpless need Freud himself could not afford to remember or imagine it. Then, there was the small child of later development turning to the father for protection. But what had happened between these two pe-riods of childhood development? Perhaps the oceanic con-sciousness had been lost in the no-man's-land that stretches between first bonding to the mother and the later relation-ship to the father? The failure of that unbounded primordial consciousness to develop in the child, alongside and com-plementary to the bounded ego, might have something to do with the way in which infants separate from the mother and gradually renounce her and finally leave her behind, as they move into the father-world and turn to him, in his awesome patriarchal authority, for his protection.

I had already read a great deal about early childhood de-velopment by the time I went down to spend a season in the underworld. I knew the theories of first bonding and separating from the mother. I had filled up notebooks of my own with jottings and speculations. But now I wanted to measure theories against my own experience. Why, I had come to ask, does the child abandon the mother-world? Why don't we hold on to it along with the father-world we later come to know? Why do we have such a formidable need to turn to the father for protection? Against what? And why couldn't the all-powerful mother of first infancy protect us? Is it that we need protection against her? Against what we feel for her?

These questions, which had unearthed themselves from my waking dream states, are actually very familiar to psychoanalytic thought. They arise within the general speculation as to why girls give up the mother as a first love object and turn to the father instead. In psychoanalytic language this great drama of choice between mother and father is called the change of object and has been written about from the very beginnings of psychoanalysis as part of the oedipal crisis through which girls pass during the long, slow movement toward "femininity."

All this had been bread and butter to me for many years. But it was not until I made my bed in the underworld that I grasped the relevance of all this to my own theme—the loss of primordial consciousness, the loss of the image of the Great Goddess, the sense of dread and resistance encountered during the initiation process when we are being drawn back toward a direct knowledge of the primal mother in all her goddesslike power.

I must have been blinded by the fact that psychoanalytic theory, discussing this urgent developmental moment in the life of the girl, had characteristically focused its attention on the sexual implications of the turning from mother to father. It talked about clitoris and vagina, passivity and receptivity, the penis, the longing for the penis, the vagina as wound. But now that I was looking up at the roots of things I realized that psychoanalytic theory of the change of object had missed the point. Hidden within the sexual-object choice there were far more momentous choices taking place that would have profound influence upon the girl's subsequent development.

In the renunciation of the early mother, this violent turn against her in favor of the father, I was able to locate the basic ground for the failure of self-development in women. For when the mother is renounced the body that loved and needed and longed for the mother must also be cast out of the self. When the infant-body with its primal needs is renounced, the primal knowledge of female power is also lost. When the primal knowledge of female power goes, we lose the inspiring image of the mother as Goddess and all memory of the time when we ourselves, wrapped up in the mother, were indistinguishable from the Goddess.

And similarly: when we turn toward the father and choose him, we enter a world of bounded ego-consciousness, with clear separations between self and other, a pronounced emphasis upon linear logic, an attitude of domination toward the body, which has come to be perceived as an enemy, for it threatens us always with its longing for return to the primal connection with the primal mother. The change of object, imagined until now as a choice between mother and father, contained within itself the original seed bed of conflict between intuition and reason, feeling and thinking, mind and body, mother as Goddess, father as God. Here was the fundamental ground of self-division I had been tracking since I first entered the valley of the frozen trees in the mountains outside of Dublin.

I had been baking myself for a long time in the mother-oven when I began to think like that. But now, wrapped in my heavy blanket, with Freud for a pillow and my own thoughts for companionship, I began to see that psychoanalytic theory had been asking the wrong questions. It had wondered why the mother was abandoned by the child, but had never once raised the question of the Great Goddess. It had talked about the movement from mother to father, but not about the loss of rapture in nature or pride in the female body. It had taken the loss of primordial consciousness to be inevitable and had not therefore given adequate reasons to account for this loss.

Nevertheless, I thought it could be worth my while to hang out for a time with these theories, since they had at least concerned themselves with the loss of the original love bond to the mother. If they had also hidden the Great Goddess and all her implications behind the preoccupation with the human mother, I might still be able to catch glimpses of the former in the theoretical statements about the primal mother and some indication therefore why the Goddess had been so thoroughly exiled during that crucial turn from mother to father in early childhood. For it seemed clear that when the primal mother was split off and banished from consciousness, the Great Goddess would also be lost. These two, linked indistinguishably within primordial experience—whatever fate the primal mother had endured would likewise have fallen to the Mother Goddess.

"The change of object is a crucial step in woman's development," Catherine Luquet-Parat has written. "It is the move in which the little girl decathects her mother as the object of love in order to cathect her father."

This great crossroads in female development involves, according to the classical psychoanalytic accounts, a violent, bitter, and absolute rejection (the decathexis) of the mother, who has thoroughly ceased to be the girl-child's love object and has become instead her rival for the father.

In later analytic thought this supremely important moment in female development was understood to be far more complex. Nancy Chodorow states this succinctly: "Such a view, while theoretically useful in its retention of views of

the feminine and masculine oedipus complex as mirror opposites, was too simple to encompass even Freud's own
work. . . . When we look at the kinds of explanations put
forth for this turning . . . we find that they testify to the
strength of a girl's on-going relationship to her mother as
much as to the importance of her relationship to her father."

Catherine Luquet-Parat is likewise concerned with the
complexity of this turning from mother to father. "Probably," she reminds us, "in view of this complexity Freud
spoke of a 'triple change' taking place during the oedipal
crisis: change of love object, change of the leading erog-
enous zone (the erotic cathexis of the clitoris yielding to
that of the vagina), and change from a position of activity to
one of passivity toward the love object." Yet, as she goes on
to note, "no two authors agree on the details of this 'triple
change' . . . Therefore the problem is always stated ambigu-
ously, further affecting our grasp of the complexity of this
period."

Many years ago, when I still naïvely assumed that girls
became heterosexual because they were intended to do so
by nature, it surprised me that psychoanalysts had felt the
need to elaborate such complex explanations for what
seemed to be an inevitable biological event. It had never
really occurred to me that girls love their mother goddess
with an intense, focused, and brooding passion long before
the father takes shape for the small child. But now that I
came to think about it from Hel's point of view, it began to
surprise me that this profound shift in love orientation took
place at all. The mother once so awesome and powerful,
source of life and nurturance, primal ground of wholeness,
present from the first moment of birth as warm body, hot
milk, sweet honey of skin touching skin. The father so
aloof and remote, so rarely present, so seldom nurturing,

so distant from the infantile body with its needs and urges. Why did the little girl ever come to choose him in the mother's place? If the change of object did not take place inevitably, as part of nature, why indeed did it take place at all?

I decided to make a huge placard of theories other people had evolved and pin them up over my little cot. In the books I read, these theories had been written in ink. But one of the belly-laughing denizens of Hel's mansion gave me a good nudge in the ribs and suggested that I had better write them in blood. They are not really fond of abstract ideas in the underworld. Down here, they give credit only to what you have dragged up, by heavy labor, out of your own veins.

These then are the theories I transcribed in blood on the placard over my little cot.

CATEGORY: Classical and revised psychoanalytic account of the reasons girls renounce the mother.

SUBCATEGORY: Penis Theories.

Straightforward Penis Theories: These range from the girl's desire to get a penis from the father for her own narcissistic pleasure (to have it on her because she wants to wield its power), to the girl's desire to get the father's penis for sexual gratification (to have it in her so that she can enjoy it). Either way, she renounces the mother when she discovers the mother's inability to provide her with the highly desirable male genital.

Oral Penis Theories: Other theorists, with an eye to complexity, include in this development the idea that the girl-child's urgent frustration with the breast leads her to reject it and to turn instead to the penis for oral gratification. The breast having failed to provide an all-fulfilling bliss, maybe the penis will provide it instead? The mother having failed to be an all-fulfilling source of gratification, the girl spurns her, thrusts her away from herself, and turns with desperate hope to the father.

Deprivation Penis Theories: Freud, founder of the penis-theory school, contributes to this account of the girl's rejection of the mother the idea of the girl's hostility toward her. The girl comes to hate her mother because the mother deprives her and because she is, by virtue of being a woman, intrinsically a powerless creature. Moreover, she arouses in her daughter terrifying sexual desires that she then compels her to renounce. What relief, finally, to give her up and turn instead to the powerful father, who encourages appropriate heterosexual desire that some other man, in his name, will one day lawfully fulfill.

Archaic Penis Theories: Later psychoanalytic theories add further refinement to this account: they note that the primal bond is characterized by primal intensity, primal frustration, primal ambivalence. The primitive nature of this first relationship to the mother, its archaic force, its passivity, they say, all compel it to be driven out of the psyche into an irretrievable oblivion. The girl turns to the father as a means of escaping from this all-terrible first mother. She looks to the man to protect her from the mother's power and from her own primitive urges. In these accounts: the penis as savior.

Potency Penis Theories: Here we move from primitive urges to the self. The mother in her power creates in her child a sense of dependency and helplessness; she wounds her child's sense of self-esteem and autonomy precisely because she, as mother, has such formidable capacities the infant lacks. Omnipotent mother; passive, impotent child turning then to the father, hoping to get his penis as a source of power and freedom from her dependence on the mother.

Mother-Love Penis Theories: In these, it is the intense, brooding, focused, passionate mother-love that drives the girl to abandon the mother when she realizes that the mother prefers men, chooses the father rather than the girl-child, and admires the little brother more than his little sister because he, like the father, has a penis. If now the little girl also turns to the father because she might hope to get a penis from him, it is not because the penis is a symbolic promise of power, but because the mother will love her better if she, too, has it.

I put up these theories on the earth walls of the underworld because I revered them greatly. Although they were all penis theories, I respected them for the subtlety of their symbolic understanding. The penis as power, the penis as nurturant symbol analogous to the breast, the penis as symbol of freedom from primal impotence, the penis as safe place of retreat from primal hostility to the mother, the penis as token of the father's awesome social power within the patriarchal world. This symbolic understanding of the reasons girls might wish to have and possess a penis I took very seriously, indeed. And I noted with particular interest the themes of frustration, hostility, forbidden desire, disappointment with the mother's powerlessness, failed mother-love. I agreed that it would take a complex motivation of this kind for a girl to give up the mother and take the father as a love object in her place.

I, on the other hand, was interested in developing a breast theory for the reasons a girl turned from the mother and chose the father instead. After all, I reasoned, the little girl once knew the primal mother as herself, and therefore could imagine herself as fated one day to develop into the awesome, breast-bearing goddess-mother the original mother once seemed. With that possibility of growth and development swinging above her, the little girl would need one hell of a motive to reject the breast and take the penis in its place. But could the penis theories possibly account for this motive when they had forgotten all about the Great Goddess?

So there I was, with this thought suddenly released from my abstract speculations and once again adrift in primordial consciousness, remembering and reliving my times at the breast. How bitterly, indeed, I had once awakened in darkness and called out screaming and kicking for my mother to come. What violence in my small legs, what passion in my hands drawing themselves into fists. It made sense to imagine, therefore, as other theorists had, that I was powerfully motivated to retreat from the archaic, disturbing, and primitive nature of this experience, to get away from the mother who could remind me of it, and turn, in hope of forgetting, to my father instead. Indeed, the penis theories had worked so well they had almost managed to persuade me there was nothing more to understand about the nature of the primal mother bond.

And yet: swimming there on my small cot I began to have other recollections of this time. Here I was now, in a state of bliss, bathed in primal blessedness as if I had not yet fully been expelled from the womb. I could actively recall the vast stretches of time during which this bliss state reestablished itself, again and again, after every disruption. I woke into cold, screaming with hunger. She lifted, she restored. I came to harbor at her breast; the bliss tide swept over me and drew me back into its sweet oblivion.

Then I remembered and lived again in those long periods of timelessness when I woke with hunger and called out to her and she did not come. I was cold and lonely, howling as I woke from sleep; yet, strangely, I seemed to be held by a female presence that did not let fear become terror for it encompassed me in a sense of breasts and arms and hovering warmth that contained my legs kicking, my mouth wailing, my body thrashing, letting me drift off into sleep again, helping my thumb find its way to my mouth, softening my harsh cries, rocking me in my small bed of not-quite-lonely being, for always there was that vast, maternal presence, who, as the poet so rightly says, "over the bent/World broods with warm breast and with ah! bright wings."

The discovery of this primordial state of well-being excited me. I wanted to shout with joy about this new experience that seemed to contradict all the theories I had myself until now formulated about infant life. Here was an archaic state of consciousness characterized not by primal intensities of need and helplessness, primitive violence, and rage, but by a sense of maternal presence.

Here, apparently, was my first experience of the Goddess-world, a domain charged with the grandeur of the primal mother, in which the question of infantile omnipotence had no need to arise, for I was rocked and soothed by an incandescent serenity that arose from within me and spread out all around me, bathing all my experience of life in a sense of dearest freshness. A bird flying over my carriage when I lay outdoors in the park, a leaf falling into my hands, my mother's face bending over me, all seemed to partake of this greatness and goodness.

Wasn't it possible, therefore, I now asked myself, that the infant had been born into the world enclosed by a primordial shield that had the capacity to protect the infant even from the failures and intrusions of the primordial mother? Perhaps archaic infant rage and alarm is, in this early phase of life, less extreme than we might have imagined, thinking of all this from the penis-theory point of view? Perhaps nature permits the human mother to fail ever and again without seriously breaking into this protective shield? Perhaps, given my own experience of the primal depths, it made as much sense to speculate about inborn serenity and bliss as inborn aggression and violence? After all, I thought, none of us can know for certain what the infant experiences in its timeless realm before articulate speech. All of us, theorists of every persuasion, are forced to reconstruct and reimagine, even when we drop down within the psyche to what seems to be a primordial ground. To speak of this experience, to work it out as theory, we are required to translate it into the verbal modalities of conceptual thought.

I was imagining an inborn state of psychic self-protection which life itself, with all its unavoidable harshness, could not easily penetrate. Certainly this idea seemed to match up much better with what I was myself experiencing, daily now, on my drifting cot. The child wrapped in a Goddess-comforter, blessedly at sea in a primal world that enclosed and contained it and allowed the human mother her inevitable incapacities to meet the capacious needs of a helpless newborn without seriously damaging her offspring or providing it with cause, later in life, to turn away from her and cast her out in favor of the father.

At this point I rose from my cot and began to fly about in my earth room. I was dissolving and coming together again, stretching my wings like a large white moth and fluttering toward the light. My thoughts, too, seemed to be winged creatures with a buzzing song. In this primordial state I had now retrieved, thinking itself became a rapture, for I now felt able to believe that the infant brought with it from the womb a condition of serenity that was the ground of all our yearning for the female and for the Goddess. On this ground, the fundamental underworld of the human psyche, rested a healing potential of mother-love and self-protection. If only we could figure out how to get back to it and why we had developed cause to cast it from us in the first place.

What? After all this writing in blood I still did not know, to my own satisfaction, why we lose track of the primal mother and cast off from ourselves the comforts of her primordial shield. Had my great flights of thought only managed to return me to the same puzzle with which my thinking had begun? Having rejected primitive violence against the mother as motive to retreat from her, having embedded archaic needs and helplessness in a Goddess-comforter that protected us even from the failures of the human mother, now that I was no longer able to put such a pronounced emphasis on infantile frustration in the mother's arms and at her breast, how was I to account for the fact that we reject her, leave her world behind, and hasten toward the world of the father?

IV

Time does not exist in the underworld. What we call years are stacked like the floors of a house, all sorts of stairways going up and down to give one access to them. I discovered that I could get back into my infant life with relative ease, sinking down into the blue nightgown my mother's friend had made for me out of her husband's discarded workshirt.

In the beginning I was always surprised to find myself in my small bed, looking up at the painted scenes of little girls and boys at play in a park. I had a pink blanket, of which I was very fond, and a small bear with a missing eye. This button-eyed creature used to share a pillow with me and keep me company whenever my mother was not there. But my life in childhood was at times bitter and disturbed. I was older now, aware that my arms came to an end at the tips of my fingers and that my mother, when she was present, stood just beyond my reach, out there, apart from me.

But what had happened to her? Who was this, adrift there beyond my grasp? Somehow she seemed to have shrunk and diminished in stature. Yes, I was older now, I saw new things in her face. There were lines and puckers on it and worried pouches; she, too, had needs no one seemed able to meet; she was confused and sometimes helpless, bending over my crib with a frown, harried and driven, barking in a loud voice, wringing her hands, looking around her urgently, calling to my sister for help. But what had she done with her luminous mantle, that incandescent beauty in which she had been dressed? What had happened to the radiant power of her Goddess-hands, moving to pick me up and enfold me within themselves? What had she done with that flowing cornucopia of potency and all-fulfillment that swayed over my head, promising me that one day I, too, would swell and be abundant and be able to nourish life?

I was looking up at the mother of my later childhood, not as she would have been seen on any one occasion, but as she gradually had come to seem over the long period of time during which what I was and she was began to be no longer exactly the same. This was the mother who had come to take the place of that primordial being that had once enveloped me, leaving her bliss shield behind whenever she went away. This mother, whose breasts seemed to have dried up and been diminished and were bound back behind layers of cloth and didn't come flowing toward me, however vehemently I demanded them.

This mother—who wanted her? This one, without doubt, was unable to meet my needs; they were so big and she so little, now that my needing arose upon the ground of a primal disappointment with her. I opened my mouth and began to wail. I had cried before now and wanted her to come and she had come and I had taken a good bite at her before I forgave her, having lost in her arms all reason to be weeping. I had cried before now and wanted her to come and she did not come and I forgave her, rocked back into the abiding sense of her primordial presence. But now, even when she stooped over to pick me up, the wailing went on and on, and the thrashing of my legs that had been split off from her body, and the rage filling my mouth that no longer grew from her all-powerful breast.

Had I turned from her because she had wounded me terribly by making me aware of her power, my impotence? Or was it because once exalted by the closeness and kinship with her potency, my participation in her omnipotence, my identity with her abundant forcefulness, I now had to face her as simply a human mother, worried, wrinkled, and used-up, the one in whom I must now soon come to read my fate as woman?

Here then was a preoedipal crisis that had been overlooked by most of the penis theories, or understood far differently by those who had attempted to account for infantile aggression at the mother's breast. Here was a crisis in which the breast was lost both as object of identification and as primary love object. Lying there, wrapped in my blanket, which no longer seemed able to keep out the underworld cold, I forced myself to live again that wound of outrage that called up my hostility at her, an unquenchable thirsty wrath at knowing her so harshly in betrayal of the female potency and creative potential she had once embodied.

She, who had once held mountains of overflowing bliss; she in whom birds made their nest, whose hair had once covered me with its radiant shield, she who had been the female ground of all possibilities, reduced now to this, the worried, the depleted, the diminished, the bound one. That was the wounding for which I could not forgive her. That was the wound that shattered prematurely the primordial bliss shield, before I was ready to grow out of it. It was this vision of the used-up mother, rather than the primal intensity of my need and desire for the primal mother, that had broken it down. I was unable to forgive her, not because she had frustrated my infantile needs, but because she had betrayed the developmental promise of the mother goddess. I was unable to forgive her, not because she was (as in

Freud) a lesser being by nature, but because she had let herself be degraded by some force or power I did not understand.

Was it possible then that those other woundings about which the penis theories had speculated were not primordial after all? Perhaps we had taken them to be so only because we could not feel or imagine our way further back? Perhaps those archaic needs were not nearly so archaic as we imagined, but were instead only the earliest portion of psyche we could reach and therefore we had assumed them to be the earliest there were? Perhaps all the issues upon which we dwell when we reconstruct the infantile experience—instinctual aggressions, archaic drives, early splitting into good and bad breast, violent frustrations, lost omnipotence, primal wounds—were actually later in development and arose only after the primordial shield had been shattered, giving way only at that moment to an unthinkable anxiety that came rushing in to take the place of the primordial bliss in which we had from birth been bathed?

At this point I stood up and began to construct another placard, written in milk, to be placed alongside the one written in blood. The crisis in human development with which I now had to concern myself was far, far older than the oedipal crisis. It arose at the moment the child became aware of itself as separate from the mother and discovered that the mother was no longer the goddess she had once been. Finally, I had glimpsed a distinctive motive for the girl's rejection of the mother, derived from the girl-child's relationship to the maternal breast as a symbol of power the mother herself had betrayed.

Here at last was a potent motive to forget the primal one, to drive her out of consciousness, to split her off and exile her in the cellars and sewers of self, where she could not remind me what a woman might be by calling up the memory of the goddess she once was. Here was the true ground of the girl's hostility toward the mother, who had betrayed the breast-power potential of the primordial female and let herself become a diminished being, her once radiant and immortal face covered now with a worried human frown.

Back to my crib: reaching out, I discovered the razor's edge where my fingertips came to an end and enclosed me lonely and separate in a hungry self. But what a world of sorrow, I now saw, lived in the underworld of the female psyche alongside this early rage of disappointment with the mother. There was my mother, a fallen and degraded being, who had once been indistinguishable from a goddess. Actively now, I could live in the pain of looking up at her and beholding her in her shrunken state. Grabbing my blanket, I willed myself to endure this agony. Pain on her behalf, knowing her as so much less than she had been. Pain on my own behalf, knowing that as she now was, she doomed me, woman-to-be someday myself, to the same dreadfully diminished fate.

No wonder I would one day go looking for my father, hoping to forget in his arms the memory of that primal one who had been lost, hoping to forget that awesome image of her which seemed, now that I saw her in her diminished guise, to diminish her yet further each time I recalled the way she once had been, her great breasts swinging, her powerful arms reaching.

In love for this diminished one I called by the name of mother, out of pity for her, and with compassion, I must forget the other one, the first one, the large one who had promised so much for being female. I must renounce, even at my own expense, all memory of what I, too, might become, in grief for this mother who had ceased to be it. I must forget the primal mother so that the diminished mother would not have to be compared to her. I must, at all costs, forget the mother goddess in order to love the human mother who peered down at me with such infinite sorrow in her dark eyes.

This disappointment with the mother for failing to be what the mother has been is a peculiarly female suffering. It sets its stamp upon the female psyche and distinguishes it, perhaps forever, from the psyche of the male. The girl rejects the mother because she has betrayed the female potential for power and development. The boy turns from the mother because he does not wish to recall the day he awoke out of the primordial bliss shield to realize that he was not a woman. This was the breast theory of human development I wrote in milk and put up on the placard above my cot.

And now I drew up my legs and put my arms around them. In the underworld this is the thinker's posture, my chin resting against my knees. The difference this retreat from the primal mother would make, much later in life, for a girl and boy seemed evident to me now. The girl, if she could discover an image or human representative of female power, would be drawn toward it, however ambivalently, in the name of her own development. The boy, confronting a powerful woman, would wish to retreat from her capacity to remind him of his primordial wound at not being woman.

Boys, it is said, pass through the oedipal crisis differently from little girls. Boys are not required to renounce the mother as primary love object, although they will renounce their claim to possess her sexually when they become aware of the father as punitive rival. But boys, as girls, must establish an identification with the parent of the same gender. At an early stage of their development, boys will have to shift their identification to the father from the mother with whom, in an early phase of merged and symbiotic being, they once identified themselves. Boys, passing through this early identity crisis, cease to think of themselves as women and take on a heterosexual orientation toward the mother.

Well, I could imagine that boys passing through this original identity crisis would wish to cast out all memory of the primal big-breasted one when they realized that they, as penis bearers, would never come to possess the bountiful, all-powerful breast. I could imagine the terrible wound at the heart of the male psyche when this awareness, slowly growing over the eons of time during which the boy-child separated from the mother, finally became a potent recognition of male difference from the mother.

To be a boy, to be forever excluded from the possibilities of giving birth, never to know the power and blessedness of creating life and nurturing it at the breast. That would be sufficient reason to cast from the self all memories and images that could remind one of this primal power one would never possess. For a boy, the image of the mother goddess would forever arouse the danger of remembering that he was no longer the same as the mother. For a boy, there would be powerful forces at work in the underworld of his psyche, to identify with the patriarchal father who rules over the subdued mother of the family domain so that he would never again have to remember his own harsh disappointment at the primal breast, once he discovered he would never bear it as his own. Clutching his penis with an anxious sense of the limitations it imposes upon him, it is nevertheless all he has to take the place of the mother-body from which he has just been separated. If now he can manage to exaggerate its significance, he may be able to persuade himself that this homuncule is an adequate replacement for the awesome female body he can never possess as his own.

I was fascinated by the current of this breast-theory speculation, which seemed to be flowing along in a way quite
different from what I might have expected from my years of
following the thrust of the penis theories. In them, development for a man-child requires a major shift in identity
but a smooth and continuous choice of love object. That is
what I, too, had always thought. Now, however, that I had
been lolling about on Hel's lap for a while, I began to wonder. Certainly, boys of the patriarchy typically leave the
mother-world earlier than girls; they make an early identification with the father, embrace more fully and less ambivalently his way of being conscious, his mode of being in
the world. Like him, they define themselves as men through
their inclination toward the mother as desirable sex object.

But on second thought I wasn't so sure. Don't men also
give up their original love bonding to that first awesome-
one, who has the capacity to wound their self-esteem by
reminding them that they are not a goddess? The boy-child
taking as love object the subordinate mother of the father-
dominated family has already fled from and renounced that
great primal mother who gave him life, picked him up wailing and helpless, giving him to understand just how fully
she had power, surrounding him with her big body and
filling his mouth with her breast-food. This all-powerful
one is not the woman men raised in patriarchy choose to
love.

Thought about in this milky way, boys not only change
identity during the oedipal crisis, they also change love object, renouncing the primal mother in fear of her power to
remind them they are not woman and not only because
they dread the father's phallic retaliatory wrath. They give
up an identification with her when they discover the penis;
they establish the subordinate, patriarchal mother as love
object in her place and identify with the father's capacity to

keep her subdued. Consequently, an underworld is created within the masculine psyche, where a mother goddess continues to preside over a primordial consciousness of relatedness to all things. Men may split off more completely this original knowledge of the primal mother; they may lose more profoundly all memory of weeping when leaves die in the fall or a deer pauses at the edge of a watering pond to lift its head and worship the Mother. They may have forgotten completely the female in themselves, having forgotten the time when their man-child body was embedded in the mother body and held the promise therefore for them, too, of one day growing breasts and a womb and bearing life and feeding it on the self-generating food of woman flesh. But within the well-defined muscularity of the ideal male physique, there is a soft, symbiotic infant curled up and waiting to remember the primal mother. In the deep underground of the male psyche the mother goddess lives on, in sorrowful exile, a denied but potent source of masculine discontent.

In this respect the male and female psyches typically evolved in our culture have more in common than we might have imagined. Both have split off and alienated, in an underworld of the self, all active memory of the primal mother goddess. Those girls who pass through the classical oedipal crisis in an appropriate "feminine" way are said to be the mirror-opposite of their little brothers. They hold the primary identification with the mother, it is said, but renounce her as sexual love object when they turn their erotic attention to the father instead. But now that I was sucking up the implications of this bosom reasoning, I had to call all this into question, too. For clearly it is not the primal mother in her abundant power with whom most girls raised in the patriarchal family identify themselves. The girl-child, passing through the oedipal crisis, rejects the primal mother, identifies with the subdued mother of patriarchy, and takes the father as love object because of his capacity to help his daughter subdue all memory of the primal mother in her full potency and power. If he can help her forget the primal mother, she will be spared all recollection of early disappointment and rage with the mother's fall from being goddess, and she will be freed from the aching pity aroused in her by the sight of the diminished, human mother.

I was moving along steadily now on my quest for answers. Here, I felt, was sufficient motive to reject the primal mother. This breast-theory speculation would account for the early splitting within both the male and female psyche with the consequent loss to both of all memory of the mother goddess. But what about those women who are said to maintain their original love bond to the mother, who take on an identification with the father, rather than with her, and who therefore become later in life the lovers of women? They are imagined never to have abandoned the mother as primary love object. Their oedipal development, thought to be parallel to that of boys, is said to bring about a change in identity from mother-likeness to father-likeness, to involve a continuous choice of love object, and to result in a psyche deemed highly inappropriate for a properly feminized woman.

And yet, upon reflection, I could see that to be lesbian is no guarantee that one has held a constant sense of mother-power within oneself or can afford to embrace the primal mother in another woman and fall back into her primal world. For the question, clearly, is not whether a woman chooses another woman as love object but in what way she is able to love her. Whether with desire to dominate, conquer, and control, as most people raised in patriarchy love women, or through a capacity to fall back into the original

symbiotic ground of first-knowledge before separations—
that ground from which the Mother Goddess arises to
guide the authentic new development of women.

To be lesbian is also no guarantee that one is able to give
herself freely in love to the mother in the other woman. For
the question clearly is not whether a woman gives herself in
love to a man or a woman, but how she gives herself.
Whether she gives herself away. Gives herself over to be
dominated. Gives more of herself than she can afford to
give and still be a self. Sacrifices more than she should in a
desire to be made whole in the self of the other or in hope
of becoming, through the other, what one can only become
through the self.

The lesbian love of women, just as the heterosexual male
love of women, may represent a longing for the mother-
world with its fierce passions and vivid sense of meaningful
existence. A man or woman may well seek in love the original image of the mother goddess and both will probably be
able to find a reflection of it in a woman more easily than in
a man. A lesbian may, in loving women, feel inspired to call
up, from the primal underworld of her own psyche, the
images and experiences that once so vividly inhabited that
dark, fertile ground. But there are no certainties here, no
assurances that this task of confronting the primal mother
would be easier for a girl in love with a girl than for a boy in
love with her.

Heterosexual women and men, lesbian women, gay
men, bisexual women and men, celibate, promiscuous,
monogamous, polygamous, women and men: we have all
passed through the Great Change in Object. And we have
all passed through it in the same direction, away from the
mother-world and toward the father-world. Away from
the fertile seed bed of inherent female power, toward the
father-dominated family, where the mother goddess of in-

fancy has become the subordinate wife and mother of the nuclear patriarchal clan. Women and men of every possible sexual orientation have passed through a major developmental crisis in early childhood, when we renounced the primal mother, drove her into exile in the underworld of the psyche, and then forgot her. To get her back again, to go in search of her, that is a universal cultural task, as necessary for men as for women, as much needed by women as by men.

In the underworld I dreamed of reversing this universal outcome of the change of object. Maybe, I thought, a woman with sufficient daring could leave the father-world and start out on a quest for the primal mother we all have lost when we leave the epic world of our first bonding to the mother and enter the domestic realm of the nuclear family where the patriarchal father rules the diminished mother and her brood.

This task, I imagined, would more likely fall to a heroine than to a hero, because for a boy the step into the father-world is a movement into patriarchal power. Taking hold of his penis, not now as a sign of sorry difference from the mother but as an emblem of male clan-membership in the father-world, he acquires a powerful tool for forgetting his earlier grief at the discovery he is not a woman. But for a girl, turning away from all memory of the breast, turning to the penis as savior, what terrible havoc. For the girl, the father-world is such a problematic choice. It may free her from maternal disappointment and pity, but it also locks her into the house of female diminishment. For the father cannot ever be what the mother once was and she herself could be, if only she were able to remember the mother goddess. So much less is expected of him in his bounded world of separate being. He who cannot give birth, he who cannot lift and return her to a paradise of symbiosis, restoring the primordial bliss shield when it has been temporarily breached, he whose chest never swelled and overflowed with life—what a terrible despair the girl must feel at having been driven, finally, to turn to him, this breastless one, and to cast out from oneself all memory of the mother goddess.

The girl-child, who might have developed a sense of female power derived from her first experience of the primordial mother; she who might therefore have been capable of an altogether natural form of creative self-expression derived from a primordial ground of wholeness and bliss, must now seek for compensatory forms of being a self. She must become obedient, where she might have been authoritative; she must come to know herself as self-effacing, where she might have been in command of herself; now she is serving others at her own expense when she might, in the image of the mother goddess, have served to remind us that woman is capable of the original act of creation.

The boy, studying the power relations of the patriarchal family, will soon be able to stanch his primordial wound at not being woman. In the father-world the boy is increasingly able to forget the female primal world that damaged him with its contrast to his more limited, male potential. Brandishing his little penis in his hand, looking up to daddy's larger instrument, he can soothe his ache at being one who will never have a breast. And so now he watches with militant attention the way his father sits at ease while mother scurries to serve him. Why should he wish to remember the mother goddess in her power? For him, it seems far better to forget, to pretend the primal world has never existed, to keep it as far from himself as possible, even at the cost of losing forever the natural rapture and kinship with the world that were once his, and that identification with all its creatures he, too, once knew, wrapped up in his safe perch in his mother's arms, bathed in a primordial consciousness that had not yet broken apart into self and other or been ravaged by the primal intensities of his primal wound at being male.

But for the girl, what a fateful move has taken place when she goes up out of the mother-world and enters the world of her father. Here in the father-world, woman as powerful has been forgotten, all memory of her has been effaced; there is no possibility here of developing, as a woman, into a being of autonomous potency. Here, for this girl-child who might be goddess, there is now only the choice of seduction or male-identification. This choice: to subordinate the self, bind the full potential of her breast-power as woman, subtly wooing and finally winning the patriarch so that she can establish a place for herself in his sphere of social and cultural power. Or instead: to take on his power in an act of imaginative identification that cuts her off even more fully from the possibilities of developing in the image of the mother goddess.

Diminished woman with bound breasts, developing so seductively in the image of her diminished mother. Pseudo-male with imaginary penis dangling between her legs. Either way, she has castrated the breast she might so proudly bear, if only she could afford to remember.

And so she hesitates, holding herself in the preoedipal world far longer than her little brother, who has given the mother a good hard push and run over to flex his muscles for daddy's approval. She hesitates, wispily recalling the primal mother who might still model for her the potentialities of her inborn female being; she fills with pride, adrift in the half sleep of not yet forgetting, drowsing in her mother's lap. She looks up, smiling blissfully, to share the newly awakened memory of the first mother with this later mother, whose hand, rough and chapped, now falls heavily on the daughter's forehead and lies there with its burden of diminishment, no longer capable of overflowing tenderness or power. This hand of the patriarchal mother: a worried hand, asking for love it cannot easily give.

The girl-child closes her eyes; she looks away, she doesn't want to see and know the mother's fall from power. Her heart aches for this mother who bends over her, brushing her forehead with her breast, evoking yet again that primal one she once was, the image rising with its incandescent power, small hand reaching for awesome breast, hungry mouth finding its Eden. Small mother and big mother so bitterly at war within this girl, who stands up finally, shoving the mother away, furious at her for reasons she cannot name or define. She leaps to her feet, she runs off in search of the father, who sits quietly at the dining-room table reading the daily newspaper. He looks up, mildly preoccupied, pleased at the way she is coyly smiling up at him as one who can help her forget the primal goddess. And now, when he pats his lap she clambers up to gaze into the newspaper with him, leans back finally, closes her eyes, and wills herself to take him in the place of the betrayed and betraying diminished mother.

This is the great crossroads of female development, when the mother is finally abandoned as primary love object and the father is established firmly in her place. This is the fateful dividing point of two worlds, each with its own imagery of what is possible for female development. A girl at this crossroads is a being torn with a harsh and implacable self-division. At this crossroads the human potential for wholeness splits in two and cannot be reunited until we are able to drop down in the underworld of the psyche and relive, on a small cot, in an earth room, the dreadful choice we were once forced to make between the mother- and father-worlds of early childhood.

Alas, the penis theories of human development do not adequately stress the female problem of self-development. The penis theories are able to imagine archaic needs, primal frustrations, disappointment with the mother as a power-less being, forbidden sexual desires, failed mother-love. But they are not able, as the breast theory of human development might be, to call up awareness of the female desire for power and capacity in distinctively female terms—for which the breast is the original and most potent symbolic expression.

But now that I had made my way back to this great crossroads, where human self-division begins in the choice between the penis and the breast, I could reinterpret the themes of the penis-theory school. Wearily, but with a promise of new energy yet to come, I climbed up out of my childhood bed and went back to writing in milk the theoretical possibilities to which I had been brought during my long sojourn in the underworld.

I saw now that the archaic intensity of the mother-daughter bond would become a motive for rejecting the mother, not because of the generalized needs and primal frustrations the daughter had felt at her mother's breast, but because of the particular wounding the daughter had experienced when she realized that her mother was unable, so far as female development was concerned, to fulfill the promise of the primordial goddess the mother had once seemed to be.

Similarly, I realized that the daughter's frustration with the mother's inability to provide her with a penis could be more accurately expressed as a frustration with the mother's limitations as a woman, in purely female terms. In this concept the mother was first measured, not against the father's social and cultural power, but against the awesome, mythological power of the primordial mother.

And again: the daughter turned from breast to penis, not because the breast had failed to be an all-fulfilling source of bliss, but because the breast had inspired a hope and trust in the female capacity to embody an abundant, free-flowing power of selfhood, which the diminished mother of later childhood had disappointed, harshly.

The forbidden sexual desires the mother was said to have aroused could, from this point of view, be understood instead as forbidden desires for self-development, forbidden when the mother herself failed to live them out and therefore aroused in the daughter a contradictory wrathful and compassionate pity on the mother's behalf, when she measured the mother against the daughter's sense of possibility, derived from her primordial image of the Great Mother.

The omnipotent mother, who was imagined to have wounded her child with the contrast between maternal power and infantile helplessness, could be seen instead to have wounded the child by virtue of the mother's own sense of helplessness with respect to innate female powers and capacities the mother could not translate into social and cultural terms of female potency.

And finally: the mother had failed to love the daughter, not because the daughter lacked the penis the mother herself admired, but because the diminished mother had come to resent and envy the unique quality of female power the daughter, as a woman, still embodies. She had failed to love the daughter sufficiently as daughter because her girl-child would one day possess the breast that inevitably represents to the older woman the mother's own failure to embody its potential.

When the daughter at the crossroads rejects her mother and chooses her father instead, it is because she cannot find within the mother-world a way to grow into the full promise of her original female being. Tragically, she rejects her mother because the older woman has rejected the Goddess. And now the daughter, who has not been taught the way to develop her true breast potential as a woman, must go looking for other forms of power instead. Unfortunate daughter, fated now to seek the power of the father-world.

V

Time was returning, it was not far away; I could feel it approaching, a great wave from out of the future. Soon, I knew, I would climb back up out of the underworld. I began to pace about in my earth room, eager for the moment when the spiral staircase would appear and I would step out into the life I had once led. I tipped back my head and gazed at the roots blooming above me, imagining the lofty trees, the low scrub, the flowers growing from them, up there in the world. I reached out and traced the roots with my hands. They were so firmly established there, entwined with one another, gripping the earth. Had I imagined my way therefore into yet another theory of inexorable woe and disorder, an inevitable deep-rooted part of female development?

I sat down on the ground and tucked up my legs. I had already, long before my sojourn in the underworld, come to understand that psychoanalytic theories must be placed in a cultural setting if we are to do full justice to human experience. Was there, then, some way to imagine that a girl-child in her growing, meeting the unavoidable stage of differentiation from the mother, beholding the older woman in her human form, could pass through this crisis without being wounded by it? What kind of mother would be required to guide her daughter through this developmental stage without marking her child with an inevitable scar? None of us, I felt, had known a mother of this kind, for we had all been raised by a mother who came to know herself as such within the father-world and who therefore brought to her role as mother expectations derived from her culture and its maternal ideal.

Nevertheless, I could imagine a woman who knew herself first and foremost as a person; a woman, therefore, who could forgive herself for frustrating her child, for failing to be present on all occasions of infantile grief, who would understand that it was an essential part of her role to teach the inevitability of frustration. A mother of this sort would have managed to free herself from the ideal of motherhood as complete surrender of self to infant exigency. This mother, successfully evolved as a self, would know that she must keep part of herself in reserve, for purposes of her own development. She would not enter into, or encourage, her child's fantasy that she should remain a goddess. But instead she would teach the more limited power of a human mother, who understands that she must gradually cease to identify herself with the earlier Great Mother of divine nurturant capacity, who has been seen as such only because the child's vision has been shaped by the presence of the primordial shield.

This mother of my imagining: she would lead her daughter through the crisis of first differentiation and new seeing, when the primordial shield has begun to wither away, losing its full intensity as the child enters more fully the mother-world of later childhood and begins to struggle with separations and differentiations. This mother would not try to fulfill the divine image of maternal abundance and would therefore be able to teach limited and appropriate frustration without blaming herself for having caused it. She would have freed herself from a sense of personal failure at being merely human and not divine. Because she had made peace with her own infantile fantasy of the divine mother, she would cease to measure herself against the preposterous expectation it held out, by implication, for the human mother. She would be able to let her daughter behold her as human because she was able to accept herself in this diminished form. Understanding her boy-child's pain at not being a woman, she would be able to remind him that deep within the stern body that will grow to manhood there is a goddess to watch over him, making him capable of tenderness, sensitivity, intuitive sweeps of thought, passages of self-surrender, moments of ecstasy that will ease his disillusionment at not being able, ever, to bear life. Then the primordial shield, from which the child has derived the notion of the mother's divinity, would not have to be prematurely shattered but could continue, very gradually, to wither away, as the child's ego emerged and shaped itself in flexible relation to it, able to sink back into it in need, in crisis, in love, in mystical rapture, in nature worship, in creative zeal, in sexual self-surrender to the primal world.

Few of us have known mothers capable of this achievement. Most of us have passed into the inevitable separation and differentiation from the mother in the arms of a woman whose worry and concern, gazing back at us when we look up into her face, reflect the fact that she continued to share with her child the expectation that she be more than any human woman is able to become.

It is from the mother's own sense of failure to conform to this divine imagery of the Great Mother that the child also comes to believe in the mother's failure. And to be, therefore, unable to forgive the mother for shrinking and diminishing and frustrating.

But now I wanted to be even more precise about the girl-child's motives for leaving the mother-world. I wanted to push beyond answers I myself gave and go on asking ques-

tions. In the underworld they are never content with the
answers you spew forth. "Okay," they say just when you
think you've arrived at some fixed and unalterable certainty, "not bad, you're on the way. Keep going. And
while you walk on, ask yourself this: Just why is the flight
to the father so extreme?" Why (to continue this infernal
questioning) are we, as women, so content to keep ourselves in the world of his values and capacities, whatever
our sexual orientation toward other women? What faces us,
terrifies us, if we try to turn back and reenter the mother-
world? Why do we move toward and then turn back from
the embrace of the Goddess?

With these questions the ground fell away from under
my feet. Was there something I had missed the last time I'd
been tucked up in this bed? I'd chewed over the possibilities of maternal disappointment, nibbled at the idea of rage
and pity, but what about guilt? Wasn't there something
about the daughter's guilt I still had to understand before I
could fully account for the reasons girls shake off the primal mother at an early age and lose, with the loss of her, all
the developmental promise of the Goddess?

I opened my eyes. Yes, there was my mother's face, still
looking down at me, her glory so fully faded now that almost no trace of it was left. And how, I asked myself,
might the girl-child looking up into her mother's face inter-
pret this withering of the mother? There in the childbed of
our brooding upon the mother we do not yet understand
biological inexorability, the child's inevitable growth, the
parent's inevitable decline. We are not old enough yet to
develop a feminist analysis of woman's destiny within the
patriarchal world. We have not yet examined the history of
female suppression as it has been practiced for thousands of
years in the father culture or pieced together theory and

surmise about the way social suppression and biology might intertwine. We are a little girl, we know as yet only the circumscribed world of mother and child, of mouth and breast, of sucking and feeding and needing and raging and soothing and needing again and feeding and sucking. And somehow, in this process, during which for eons of timelessness the mother has remained whole and been able to support the primordial shield and to bring forth food from her ripe breasts, something has happened that has diminished the mother, caused her food to dry up, caused her to look shrunken and worried, not at all now like that primal one of awesome endowment and magical capacity.

What has happened to her? How has it come about that the abundant primal goddess has turned into withered worried mother? What could account for it? Where could the blame lie?

These were terrible questions; they carried the urgency of dawning consciousness of self, as if with these concerns about the mother my female psyche first organized itself as ego and came to know itself as separate from mother and world. For what else is there in that early world besides the mother and her child? What could have changed the mother if not the child? Yes, it must have been the child with her needing and feeding and sucking and biting who did it. She did it? She did this to the mother, causing her to shrink, to dry up, to wither, to run dry? It was I who had sucked up and drained out of my mother the primal goddess? I?

Diminished mother, guilty child: it was this lamentable condition I discovered at the heart of the female psyche when I dared open myself to the implications of the breast theory I had begun to evolve in the underground. Clearly now, I saw that this plight would inevitably lead a daughter to the crossroads, where the father-world looms up in the far distance, promising relief from the guilt of imagining that the power of the primal goddess has flowed out of the human mother's breast into her hungry child.

This crisis of differentiation from the mother reveals the mother to be different from the way she had been in two respects. Now, the mother is no longer identical with the primordial Wonder Woman. And simultaneously she is no longer the same as the little girl who looks up at her. The mother has been diminished; the little girl has grown in stature. The goddess has moved out of the shrunken mother and come to dwell with her growing child. Her legs reach farther down under her blankets; she is about to outgrow the small cot; her favorite red sweater that last year was too big doesn't button over her chest. The girl is now in possession of a power her mother no longer has. There she is, growing child standing on her own two legs, striding about commanding the small world of her life with articulate speech. She is the one in whom the primordial goddess has come to live.

The little girl, who gazes up with newly awakened eyes, sees the human mother diminished not only with respect to the primal goddess, but with contrast to the daughter's own developmental possibility. The mother has just lost the daughter to her newly emergent sense of self. And therefore, if the girl-child wonders how this power has come to move from mother to child, she will be likely to account for it by blaming herself. It is she who sucked up the primordial potency from her mother's breasts, draining the breast of its primal power, taking it into herself.

While the daughter remains in the mother-world she is torn, therefore, with a terrible guilt and finds herself in a considerable dilemma. If, on the one hand, she casts out from herself all memory and experience of the primal goddess, she consigns herself to follow in her mother's fate, for she will have lost all memory of other possibilities for the female. In the mother-world, when the goddess has been expelled, the only possibility of development that remains for the small girl is a mother who tragically embodies the entire patriarchal history of female suppression and impoverishment. In the mother-world of later childhood, when the mother has stepped out of the mythic dimension and been placed in the family kitchen, the possibility of meaningful development, as a woman, has ceased for the little girl. But if, on the other hand, she now allows herself to develop according to the original promise of the primordial goddess she must do so, as she imagines it, at the mother's expense and without the mother as companion or guide.

If the father-world holds promise for the female child, it is because in her father's house there will be no Great Mother against whom the human mother must be measured. In the father's house the girl-child will find a full forgetting of original female power—a forgetting she urgently requires if she is to cease blaming herself for the human mother's fall.

"You are Goddess," women say to one another. Grown up now, taking hands with one another in the ritual circle, they have gathered to bring themselves back into the presence of female power. "You are Goddess," each woman says to the woman standing next to her. And each time I hear these words something inside me shrinks back with an uneasy sense of guilt. Yes, I say to myself, I may be Goddess. But what about my mother?

The daughter, setting out later in life to become one with the Goddess, to regain her original sense of female power and capacity, leaves behind a subordinate and diminished woman, called by the name of mother. She cannot take this woman with her on her quest, for this woman who has spent her life within the father-world rarely is able to leave it behind and respond to the Goddess call that sets her daughter off on the path to initiation. And so the daughter, wandering around among tall trees and falling stars, becomes exalted, worships a stone, hesitates, retreats in fear, sits down and covers her face with her hands, weeping. To love the Goddess seems to her a betrayal of the mother, who once was Goddess. To become one with the Goddess reawakens in the daughter the archaic idea that she becomes Goddess at the mother's expense.

Psychoanalysis placed within a cultural setting, theory relocated in the recollection of infantile experience. This was the way, I thought, to understand the wounding at the heart of the female psyche as culturally determined and conditioned rather than as inevitable.

And so we come back to the daughter at the crossroads. It is an overcast and brooding day; dark clouds lower the sky, a crow calls its cry of desolation from a bare tree, takes to wing, swoops down over the dry cornfield. Through the woods: shaggy winter headed for its hibernation.

The daughter hesitates, looks down the road that leads back to the mother. She sees the older woman gazing at her with a frown in which the daughter, ever guilty, reads the mother's anguish at losing her child. But why is this woman frowning? She knows her daughter is about to choose the father-world that has already cost the mother herself so dearly. Does she wish the girl to endure the same fate? Does she want to stop her, to call out and warn her?

The child looks farther back. She sees in the distance the Great Mother of Female Possibility, whose image dwarfs yet more completely the worried woman in an apron whose audible, ambivalent sigh the daughter hears as she turns away toward the City of the Fathers, where her brothers have already gone to live.

And so we come upon one final twist in the unraveling thread that leads the daughter out of the mother-world. The guilt this girl-child feels toward the older woman, for having stolen her power, for diminishing her, for leaving her, for leaving her behind to her fate, now transforms her perception of the mother, who, as the daughter walks from her, comes step by step to seem monstrous and terrible because the girl-child fears her retaliation. Now she scarcely dares to look back, to face this mother she is leaving behind: in reality worried and aproned, dwarfed, ambivalent and diminished; in fantasy monstrously dangerous to the child and possessed of an awesome power to wreak revenge. And so, by the most tragic irony, the girl-child, guilty at leaving the mother, partially restores to the older woman some of her lost primal magnificence. The Great Goddess, purveyor of the primal bliss shield, rises again, but now in a fully negative and terrifying form. She is the mother who frowns when her daughter is excited, grows cold when the girl makes plans to go out with her friends, doesn't show interest in the daughter's drawings, is too busy to listen to the story she is telling, pats her on the shoulder, encouraging her to give up her dreams, to take some easier path in life, secretly telling the girl not to surpass her. Woman has become the bitch, the devouring mother, the nasty shrew, the castrator of ambition, the one who casts the evil eye.

No wonder the girl flees in terror toward the father's arms.

She does not yet know, this daughter of the mother-world, that her fate in the patriarchal city will be so vastly different from her brother's. She imagines that the father who stands along the road, bearing full cultural empowerment, will open his arms to her, too. She has no idea that she will be asked to bind her breasts and renounce their symbolic potential in return for the promise of social and developmental privilege for which his penis has become the inevitable symbol. She cannot yet imagine that in this world, where the father and her brothers will be permitted to develop fully their social power, she will be asked to develop as a woman in ways that do not frighten them with the reminder that women, too, have a way to become powerful beings. She doesn't know yet that they are muscularly phallic because they are protecting themselves from a distinctively male form of primal wound, which they must at all costs keep her from awakening. She must not remind them that there is value in female being, for she might cause them to remember how bitterly they once suffered envy and outrage when they discovered that they were not women.

She walks on, knowing only that the man who stands waiting for her seems so infinitely more capable of self-development than the mother she leaves behind. And now, as she walks toward him, she imagines his power as even greater than it is, for she thinks of him as one who has managed to subdue the Bitch Mother.

At the great crossroads of female development, when the mother-world is being renounced, the girl idealizes the father's power. She is driven to this idealization, not only because she believes the father will give her the chance for self-development, but because she urgently needs to escape her own guilt and terror at diminishing the mother she leaves behind.

In the father-world, where woman is tolerated only as subordinate wife, the power relations between mother and father help the growing girl to forget that she once blamed herself for the mother's diminishment, saw her as a revenge mother, and fled from her in terror. For a growing girl in patriarchal culture it will become a welcome thought to imagine that the father has power sufficient to subdue a primordial goddess. The father, transposed in fantasy as she turns toward him to escape the mother, becomes the heroic monster-slayer whose story has been told over and again in patriarchal myths.

For this is what power means in the father-world. The capacity to conquer and subordinate everything once associated with the Great Mother. It means conquest of the body and its primal urges, it means control over powerful feeling states that threaten always to return one to the mother's domain. It means the superman of self-discipline and self-overcoming, who proves to himself over and again how thoroughly he has mastered his need for woman, his fear of woman, his primal desire to be woman.

But for the girl-child entering the father-world, power means an eventual self-tyranny that requires the suppression of the female body. For the girl-child setting off down the road to the father, this kind of power established over the natural world of the body and its memories, means the creation of a hungry self.

The daughter born into the patriarchal family comes to the crossroads. She hesitates, looking back down the road that leads to the mother-world she is leaving, perhaps forever. She closes her eyes, unable to tolerate the bewildering imagery with which she has clothed the nakedness of the human mother. And now she begins to run to the father, faster and faster into the arms of this domestic Theseus who has managed to bring down the Revenge Mother along with the Great Goddess and to establish this dominated woman in their place. Finally now, she casts out one part of this divided image of the female that has caused her so much guilt and fear and self-reproach and sadness. Finally now, in the name of the safety and power promised by the father-world, she splits off the image of the Goddess that alone could guide her unique development as a female. If now she remembers the primordial mother at all, it will be only as a terrible monster whom the father has slain. Now, tragically, the Great Goddess, original image of female potency, is used to embellish and exaggerate the father's power.

VI

The little girl, who might develop into the Woman Who Is Not Yet, needs a mother who remembers the Goddess.

A mother who is able to initiate the daughter, through acts of remembering, into an awareness of those primordial images that are the daughter's birthright.

A mother who rocks her daughter against her breast and tells stories about the Goddess.

A mother who shapes the Sabbath challah in the form of a breast and reminds her daughter that German Jews called the loaves of twisted Sabbath bread "berches," derived from Berchta, the old German goddess of vegetation.

A mother who teaches her daughter the sacredness of giving birth, reminds her of the miracle that occurs when food springs forth from female flesh.

A mother who sings to her girl-child the African lullaby of Ymoja, sister of the fishes.

A mother who remembers the ritual of preparing and offering food, who recalls that women once knew the power of healing.

A mother who remembers that women were warriors and judges, scholars and scribes.

A mother who knows that Hel is the house of the Goddess, that Hel's regenerative fires bring rebirth, creative passion, fiery selfhood.

A mother who feeds us pomegranates, who hopes we

will eat the seeds and stay for a long time in the underworld where she, too, has been, visiting with Persephone.

That a mother of this kind would be hard to find in a patriarchal family setting, with its limited view of female being, should not surprise us. But it also should not make us despair. For brooding there, in the underworld of the human psyche, a powerful goddess lies in wait for us, calling to us from out of her banishment, luring us back, singing to us in her siren voice, asking us to remember.

She requires us to live again in the pain of knowing the mother's decline and fall from power. (She who was very large has become much smaller.) She asks us to remember the first time we opened our eyes to behold the face of the diminished mother. (She grows old, she grows old.) She requires us to face the revenge mother we have built up out of our guilt and remorse at abandoning the mother. She asks us to face the terrible knowledge of woman's fate within the father-world and to cease blaming ourselves for it, finally. Then she will open her arms to us, will speak to us from a burnt tree, from a rose petal falling at our feet when we leave the garden, and this time we will walk into her embrace, without dread of her power to make us remember.

Part Four

DISOBEDIENCE

*I am the one whom they call Life and you have
called Death
I am the one whom they call Law and you have
called Lawlessness
I am the one whom you have pursued and I am
the one whom you have seized.*

—The Thunder, Perfect Mind

I

I dream: I am climbing a spiral staircase. It is winding up
from the underworld. I carry a heavy blanket, a folding
cot, a placard, a few charred books, a handful of mud.

I reach my study; the window is open. It is a spring day;
a squirrel is walking about on my papers, smearing the ink
that has not dried since I lifted my pen, closed my eyes for
a moment, descended into the underworld.

I sit down quietly at my desk. The squirrel scampers
away. I start to work with the lump of earth I have brought
back from Hel's kitchen. I become aware of a voice. It has
been speaking since I began to climb the spiral staircase. I
took it for a soft humming with something of lullaby,
something of love song. Yet now, as I prop up the clay
figure on my desk, the voice says: "This is the New Eve.
The Woman Who Is Not Yet."

My heart begins to pound. I wake up fully. The squirrel
has vanished, my papers are stacked neatly on my desk.
But my hands! They are covered in mud.

This won't do, I say to myself. It wasn't only a dream. I
have been there. I haven't returned empty-handed to my
life. The past exists; I have entered it. I have gone back and
rocked myself awake in the arms of the primordial mother.
This loneliness, I tell myself, this sense of desolation, exists
because I am afraid to take up the task that has been en-
trusted to me.

I pick up my pen. I begin to write. It grows dark while I sit bent over my papers. I don't lift my head to turn on the light. A faint glow has been hovering over my desk, illuminating my work. I thumb through the papers, with their crossed-out lines and scribbled words. What have I written? I lean over to look more closely. It is a poem cycle. It has a title. It is called: "The Uncertainty of Eve."

I. *Sleep*

> I wait, but do not wish to hear you call
> Fearing you shall awake, one night
> out of the centuries, to wonder
> what became of that form
> stretched out by evening at the center of the world.
> And what shall I make of the fact
> that all things, coming towards me,
> seem myself? Shall I
> fall on my knees, as I wish?
> In a gesture, shall I call it despair?
> Or is it you, smoothing a path for me:
> urgent, imperative:
> even in sleep?

II. *The Awakening*

> Intended for Eden,
> how did you keep the waters innocent
> of the awakening that is rain?
> Or the herbs of the field
> before they grew?
> Or the mist that arose
> out of its own necessity
> to anoint the earth?

III. *The Call*

Was I summoned?
Or did I rise
from my own emergency?
Dreaming of a dark and formless thing
that had no eyes
and fashioned mine.
Remembering:
waters, the disquieting wind
dark earth and the dismembering fire.
A servile arc
that roared disquietude,
wakened from slumber;
and breath,
ribbed with mortality.

IV. *Silence*

Listen with the far side of thought.
Bewildered, something speaks to us
Ruins the spring's dynastic hope
and wrings through summer for a savage eloquence
we, hastening after shadow, cannot hear.

V. *Gardens*

I do not want you in beauty
disordering truth
or preaching the measures
of your runic tongue.
You, who walked in the garden
instructing the winds
discover me
as I would know you:
naked as light.

VI. *Breath*

> Carefully blending
> with malice of yewberry
> patience of lebanon's cedar
> the dark, with disordered
> of sycamore's shadow
> with brave, the unbroken
> in vigilance bowing
> the cypress
> to wandering breath of an evening.

VII. *Surrender*

> Tomorrow
> I shall surrender
> to all the temptations
> I failed to acknowledge;
> awaken
> the serpent out of the dust
> to offer the apple
> bitten through with impatience
> for burnt
> knowledge of desire.

VIII. *Memory*

> The wind
> that wandered the garden
> arousing the dust.
> And the cry, was it rage
> when they went down in heat?
> And still, at evening
> raucous from the garden
> we recall that time
> before the rivers were divided

or the eastward portion staked
for our imperative discontent.

IX. *Ritual*

Subjected to the light
we may no longer hope
for dark among the shadows
long though fall the measure
of a day's despair.
And comfort rises from a certainty
more settled now than sorrow:
upon the leaf, this tribute
veined and importunate.
Upon the pool, this breath
a ritual of light.

X. *After the Fall*

For the survivors
a gathering was planned.
They served us water from the dead sea
and bread of that fine, old wheat
no hand had planted
in a soil grown bitter
with the camel's tread.
A wind rose up between us
like new wine. And we
were silent,
in the shelter of time at last.

XI. *Knowledge*

You who despise the mask
assume the shape of our ancestral images:
The great ice warrior descended from the peaks

In conquest of the desert sand.
And when you trace that line
upon the cave's observant rock
a reindeer pauses in the chase
and we crouch down, our arrows raised,
upon the edge of thought.

II

It took me a long time to understand the Eve poem I wrote when I came back out of the underworld. For years I returned to the poem, read it over, puzzled it out. Eve, the original sinner, violator of the primal taboo against eating, responsible for the corruption of Adam and for the Fall. What could she have to do with the Woman Who Is Not Yet?

But one night, when I was at work on my novel, *The Flame Bearers*, about a sect of women that worships the Goddess, I realized that for them Eve would not have been a sinner. When they sat down at night to tell her story they would have called up a woman who had broken a patriarchal taboo against forbidden knowledge. For them, Eve would have been a woman who awakened in a garden ruled over by the Father God and realized that something was withheld from her in that world where she was expected to be subordinate to her husband.

I reached for the poem cycle I had written many years earlier, read it over once again, and realized that my Eve had addressed herself not to the Father God but to the Great Mother. It was she who had been sleeping for centuries, leaving her mud work, her attempt to shape the Woman Who Is Not Yet, unfinished at the center of the world. The dark and formless thing was all that remained of the Mother Goddess when this female lump of earth awoke

—an eyeless, unshaped *prima materia* from which all life nevertheless was formed, part water, part air, part earth, part fire.

My Eve understood that to get back to the knowledge of original creation she must listen with the far side of thought, to voices that speak in savage eloquence, with the naked presence of light, directly to intuition. She vowed to awaken the serpent, to go after the apple bitten through with impatience for burnt knowledge of desire.

The Eden in which Eve was born was only a partial truth; a story she needed to complete by a return to the spontaneous ritual of the natural world, reading the leaf's wisdom and the pool's ceremonial presence. New wine, old wheat, virgin soil not yet beaten down by trade, time sheltering the survivors for whom the dead sea still held fresh water—my Eve knew something about the expulsion from Paradise that had not yet been told. She had a knowledge that encompassed our most ancient ancestral images. This was the Eve, the New Eve, I had brought back with me from Hel. Here precisely was the woman I had begun to conceive in the underworld, the culture-heroine who one day will set out on the epic quest I had imagined, leaving the father-world in order to retrieve the long-lost primordial mother.

It was all there, but what could I do with it? How could I dare to imagine that Eve, in whose name women for so long have been associated with sin and its punishment, was actually a heroine? That the curse uttered against her might have been a blessing in disguise? And why Eve? Why not some other figure whose reputation had not been so thoroughly besmirched?

Yet I felt sure that Eve had come back with me from the underworld intentionally. The transformation of woman is a work of archetypal dimension and significance. To change fundamentally the nature of woman, it would be necessary to transform the archetype itself. To imagine Eve, the sinful first woman, as rebel in Paradise, is itself a bite into the forbidden fruit. She, who has been used to warn us against our headstrong tendency to do things our own way, no matter what authority is threatening us with punishment. Eve, who had been used to chastise us if we sought knowledge, now transposed into the figure who tempts us to seek it?

I began to look through my library, wondering if I could come up with a version of Eve that matched my own, but for the longest time I found only the familiar references and soon my head was filled with odd bits of poetry, quotations, folk sayings, and fragments, all of them telling the same tale.

There was Milton, for instance, describing Eve when she ate the fruit. "Her rash hand in evil hour/Forth reaching to the fruit, she pluck'd, she eat:/Earth felt the wound, and Nature from her seat,/Sighing through all her works, gave signs of woe/That all was lost."

Was I really going to set out now to show that Eve's hand, reaching for the fruit, had not been a rash hand or the hour evil? That earth had not been wounded, but restored? That everything had been gained rather than lost? That Eve's supposed sin was instead her virtue?

Then there was the old Jewish folk saying I had recently come across again. "Adam's last will and testament read: 'Don't believe Eve's version.'"

But that is precisely what I wanted to do. I wanted to discover and believe Eve's version of the Eden story. I wanted to tell of woman's imperative disobedience to patriarchal law.

Yet it wouldn't be easy. "A woman has the form of an angel," says a German proverb, "the heart of a serpent and the mind of an ass." That sort of thing is what I, too, had always heard about women, who were derived from Eve and her unfortunate venture. "What could Adam have done to God that made him put Eve in the Garden?" a Polish proverb asks. The great poets, folk wisdom, all aligned against my view that there was something altogether wholesome about eating the apple. "Adam ate the apple and our teeth still ache." That is how, from time immemorial, they have thought about it in Hungary.

I was beginning to get cold feet. No, I told myself, it's just not possible that your Eve was on the way to enlightenment when she bit into the apple, that her disobedience to God was a larger form of loyalty to herself. Martin Luther, for instance, had consigned her to the uttermost category of misery: "Eve exceeded all women in sorrow and misery," he wrote. "Never came into the world a more miserable woman; she saw that for her sake we were all to die."

The Talmud, too, seemed quite definite about the nature of Eve. "It is easier to appease a male than a female—because the first man was created out of dust, which is soft, but the first woman was created out of bone, which is hard."

Well, that gave some hope, anyway. Eve, the unappeasable. I liked her in that form. It made sense that our culture-heroine would have to be bone hard in her determination to find out what she is not supposed to know. There would have to be something relentless in her insistence that woman's knowledge is not punishable.

And maybe it was precisely this unappeasable quality that had led Tertulian to claim, addressing women, that "the judgment of God upon your sex endures even today; and with it inevitably endures your position of criminal at the bar of justice. You are the gateway of the Devil."

Eve as gateway . . . but perhaps not to the Devil? Perhaps to knowledge? Daring? A wisdom we have scarcely begun to retrieve? Perhaps Eve's expulsion from Paradise was the precondition for her self-creation, the firm ground on which she who was called woman would now name herself?

Well, why not? There must have been something about Eve, more than the fact that she ate food she wasn't supposed to eat, which has caused the wise men down through the ages to keep measuring all subsequent generations of women against her. "As regards the individual nature," St. Thomas Aquinas had once said, "woman is defective and misbegotten." To which John Knox had added: "Nature doth paint them to be weak, frail, impatient, feeble and foolish; and experience hath declared them to be unconstant, variable, cruel and lacking the spirit of counsel." "If once you find a woman gluttonous," Samuel Johnson had written, "expect from her very little virtue."

Without doubt, these statements carried the authority of the ages, of powerful and enduring patriarchal tradition. But they were, on the other hand, mere human utterance. One could perhaps suppose that a female tradition, of the kind I imagined in my novel, a sect of women telling its stories in secret at the ritual bath, from mother to daughter when men were absent, would have seen Eve in a different way and with equal validity. They might have viewed her gluttony as an insatiable need to create the female sex out of woman's hunger for self-knowledge. They might have conceived Eve's fall as a rise to power. After all, Eve is a figure in a story, a character in a tale, embroidered with certain threads and particular colors, in folk sayings and philosophical papers, in ancient hymns and scholarly broodings. Why shouldn't it be possible that other traditions would use other colors and threads?

I had learned, snuggling on Hel's lap, to take Freud as a pillow instead of incontrovertible doctrine. Maybe I would now find out that the Bible, far from being God's Word or the last word, was instead an ancient collection of old stories, gathered from here and there, pieced together after every sort of fashion and filled with contradiction, the way old stories always are?

III

Jews have been telling stories for thousands of years. In the beginning, they didn't think of these stories as Holy Writ or any kind of inspired word. They were watering their oxen, it was a hot day, they got tired and looked around for a fig tree. Someone brought out a goatskin of wine; there were figs and fresh cheese, a loaf of bread and a story. They were talkers then; their schools were the village well and the spinning wheel and the things that happened when someone tied a goat under a tree and went off coveting his neighbor's wife. They told stories that could be repeated, not exactly as they had been told the first time, but with every sort of new detail and variation. A story was everyone's property, although some people told stories better than others and soon the others wanted these tale bearers to tell them again.

For a long time there was no need to write the stories down. People had good memories in those days; they listened while they worked, sharpening a scythe, gleaning rye, carding flax, forgetting themselves in the labor of their hands, drinking in the words to repeat them later, beating clothes on the rocks next to the river. They took in an old tale as if it had never been told. Living through the events without knowing their outcome, no matter how many times they had lived these events before. Filled with a nearly unbearable suspense. Wondering if Eve was going to go after that apple, where the snake came from, how Eve spoke to it, whether God would punish her, whether this time Adam, by nature slow and obedient, might finally be interested in the apple himself. Each time hearing something new in the most familiar tale. Living in this paradox that creates the tale all over again, in the space between listener and teller, where the always new, the already ancient, the never heard before, and the familiar together unfold the inexhaustible meaning of the story.

Of course, no one knows exactly when these stories began to be written down. Some books of the Bible seem to have been written by individuals, others by colleges of scribes and schools of priests. It was a long, slow process and it went on over many generations, while tales continued to be told and changed and retold and worked upon by folk imagination and ingenuity before they got into the hands of a sedentary man who set down the version that most appealed to him. So that, finally, on every page of writing, there came to be an untold number of village wells and spinning wheels and babes rocked at the breast and fig trees and loaves of bread. And all this allowed to be a not quite orderly process, during which a national literature came to be forged out of earlier and yet earlier legends.

For these ancient tales, traveling from Assyria and from Greece and from Arabia and from Chaldea and from Babylonia, had made their way into stories told by the Jews, following the camels and resting with the traders and watering themselves at the wells and getting involved with the bread baking, while Sennacherib nearly captured Jerusalem and the angels of the Lord went out and smote in the camp of the Assyrians and Manasseh paid tribute and the Chaldean conquerors subdued and the Medes troubled Babylon and the religious revival under Elijah and Elisha broke up the coalition of Israel with Syria.

So that, by our time, it was quite easy to see, once one began to chip away at the awesome authority of the mono-theistic editors, that woven into every name and character and place and event referred to in the Bible, there were stories within stories upon stories, telling these most famil-iar things in the strangest, least familiar ways.

For instance, many people had considered Eve a God-dess. She was also said to have created the serpent, a living phallus, for her own sexual pleasure. Other people said that the Goddess and the serpent were their first parents. Most people put the Goddess together with a serpent. Nidaba, scribe of the Sumerian heaven, sometimes took the form of a serpent altogether. Ninlil, who had first figured out how to plant seeds in the earth, had the tail of a serpent. On Sumerian tablets, the Goddess was called Great Mother Serpent of Heaven.

In the Greek myth, Eurynome, Goddess of All Things, "rose naked from Chaos, divided sea from the sky, danced upon the waves, stirred up the wind, was impregnated by it in the shape of a great serpent named Ophion . . . and laid the World Egg."

The serpent in these old tales is the Goddess Herself or her creative aspect and sometimes, in later stories, the snake was regarded as the Female Spiritual Principle, an Instructor, who comes to teach and inform.

All this was fascinating, of course, since it allowed me to imagine that my desire to make of Eve and her eating some-thing other than John Milton and John Knox and Martin Luther and the priestly scribes had made of her might, after all, be not so very daring as I had supposed, but could be seen instead as the oldest tradition of storytelling.

Take the fruit tree, for example. It, too, had been around for a long time all over the world, growing apples and figs and peaches and pomegranates. In China, Great Mother

Hsi Wang Mu ruled over the garden of magic peaches in the west, where gods were said to be reborn. In Greece, they told about the Goddess Hera, who had a tree of golden apples, around which the serpent Ladon coiled. Egyptians painted the Goddess Hathor within her tree, "passing out its sacred fruit to the dead as the food of eternity, immortality and continued life . . ." In a mural at Knossos a fig tree stands beside the sacred altar.

"The Great Goddess is everywhere the ruler over the food that springs from the earth . . . For this reason the great mother is frequently associated with a vegetative symbol . . . Flowers and fruit are among the typical symbols of the Great Mother."

It doesn't seem to matter which fruit grows from the sacred tree; the stories are not particular in this regard. But these old tales have a decided tendency, whoever plants, whoever harvests, whoever tells, to place goddess and tree together and to regard the tree and its fruit as sacred, an aspect of the Mother Goddess from which one is permitted to eat.

"As tree of life, the great tree Goddess of the night sky and the underworld feeds the dead, and as the 'suckling's tree' of the Aztecs she feeds the dead in the underworld with her milk."

The Babylonian Ishtar, the Great Mother, could transform herself into the divine fig tree Xikum, "the primeval mother at the central place of the Earth." Is that why Adam and Eve, after they had eaten the apple, covered themselves in fig leaves? In Goddess clothing? As a sign of loyalty, now that they had figured out who she was?

Apples, peaches, pomegranates, figs: fruits dealing out life after death, offering renewal, keeping gods and kings immortal, bringing about resurrection, representing sacred marriage, standing for knowledge that has come to be forbidden. Apparently, from these old tales and their fruitful symbols, I could take my pick.

Weaving serpent and fruit tree and first woman and primal hunger into a tale that seemed to do justice to the ancient meaning of these images, I could talk about Eve eating the apple because she knew perfectly well it was the flesh and fluid of the Goddess. Certainly that's what the apple meant for the Egyptians. Why shouldn't Eve have known their story as well as the biblical tale? Eve, born into the patriarchal garden of the biblical scribes, might very well have been hungering for the Goddess Feast that has come to be forbidden by a patriarchal God who wishes to pretend he is the only creative power in the universe. Well, why not? Perhaps Eve gave in to the snake because she had figured out the snake would take her back to the Mother Tree? Eve has been so many things to so many people. Why shouldn't she come to be for us, who are hungering for the Woman Who Is Not Yet, a rebel who put the apple in her mouth because she yearned to be reunited with the Goddess through a sacred feast that would restore to her the knowledge that, long before she awoke in the house of the Father, she had been, from the very beginning, her Mother's daughter?

IV

Every day now, as I sat at my desk, I saw the mud-pie woman changing. She was looking fit, she had a healthy glow to her. She was beginning to breathe new life into herself. She was proud of her body. Her breasts had settled into a ring of massive fruit on her chest. That, I thought, is a good indication that the woman we are creating will have an abundant capacity for self-nurturance.

Then I noticed: the lump of underworld mud had acquired muscular arms. No doubt from digging—down into the earth to recover her past.

She wore fig leaves for hair, her arms were covered in a soft bark, her eyes were bright cherries. But her legs had remained recognizably human and I understood that she had been practicing the pole vault, getting ready to leap over the walls of her father's garden.

Good for her, I thought. Now all that remains is to give her the heart of a mother lion guarding her cubs. She'll need that, I imagined, to stand guard over the next stages of her development.

At this point the snake began to twine itself around the New Eve's chest, biting at her breasts. What is that snake up to, I wondered? What exactly does it want Eve to understand? I observed, during this time, that my breasts were aching and throbbing, as if they were filling with milk. It was uncanny work, creating a New Eve out of myself. I needed help; I couldn't do it alone.

I decided to leave my house. Maybe I would run into a burnt tree and be pulled down to my knees? Or someone might bring me a glass of mint tea. Perhaps there was an unexpected child guide waiting for me at the corner? Or a few survivors of the underworld, having a good belly-laugh. Surely, I hadn't come this far with my lump of mud only to find that I could not inscribe her with the snake's wisdom?

I took the little clay figure with me, in the breast pocket of my shirt. I strolled down Telegraph Avenue and wandered around in the bookstores. If inspiration is going to strike, I thought, it will be haphazardly. And then, one day, when I was sitting in my favorite coffee shop, I put the little figure down next to my cappuccino.

A man came over to my table. I had noticed him before, over the years. He was a habitué of this place where I had written the first drafts of all my books and where dope dealers, students, professors, avenue craftspeople, street people, bag ladies came in for coffee or to eat scraps left on the plates before they were cleared from the tables. He, too, was a scribbler. We made a comfortable pair, the two of us bent over our notes and pages, letting our coffee grow cold while we worked.

The place was always crowded at breakfast time. We had found ourselves at the same table before now. This time we began to talk. He was a professor of ancient Mideastern languages; he knew Ugaritic, the language spoken in Canaan before the Hebrew conquest. "Tell me," I said to him, "what do you know about Eve and the Garden of Eden? I've read every book I could get my hands on. But something's missing. What haven't I read? Is there some mythological or religious tradition in which Eve wasn't seen altogether as a sinner or a goddess?"

I had a few errands to run before I went home. By the time I got there my new acquaintance had left a message for me on my answering machine. It was brief and cryptic. Fortunately, I recognized the voice. "There is something waiting for you at Moe's Bookstore," it said. "Ask at the desk for the literature on the Gnostic Gospels."

And so it began, from a chance meeting with a stranger in a coffee shop. That night I stayed at my desk until shortly before dawn. I read quickly, without making notes, drinking in this extraordinary world of the Gnostic Gospels, early Christian texts that had been suppressed during the formative years of Christianity when, in the middle of the second century, they had been denounced as heresy by the orthodox church. I found out that the possession of these remarkable writings (which consisted of poems and teachings, secret gospels, philosophic treatises, guides to magic and mystical practices, and strange retellings of ancient myths) had, by the fourth century, come to be a criminal offense. And so they had been buried in caves in Nag Hammadi in Egypt, where they would remain hidden and forgotten until the end of the Second World War, when an Egyptian peasant had struck a red earthenware jar and discovered thirteen papyrus books, bound in leather. At first, he had been afraid to break the jar. But he soon took heart, lifted his mattock, and brought it down on the red jar so that golden particles, which might have been papyrus fragments, swirled out of it and disappeared into the sky.

The Gnostic writings were the transitional ground of storytelling I had been seeking. With their help I would be able to decipher the snake's coded bites at Eve's breast. The

Gospels had emerged within Christianity and Neoplatonism, until both excluded them as the "heresy" of Gnosticism. They had undergone the same hazard endured by the texts of the Old Testament, having been transcribed generation after generation, from increasingly corrupt copies. But these texts delivered into my hands tales about the origin of the human race that would help me tell Eve's story as an account of women's necessary disobedience—a tale of wisdom seeking.

The Gnostic Gospels remembered the Mother.

For instance, certain Gnostic sects who believed they had inherited a secret tradition from Jesus and James and Mary Magdalene worshipped both the Mother and Father. "From Thee, Father, and through Thee, Mother, the two immortal names, Parents of the divine being," they prayed.

The Mother appears in Gnostic texts as "a great Intelligence . . . a female which produces all things." She is Holy Spirit, mother of everything, who existed before them all.

In Gnostic teaching Paradise was regarded as womb.

"Grant Paradise to be the womb," Simon Magus writes, "for Scripture teaches us that this is the true assumption when it says, 'I am He that formed thee in thy mother's womb' . . . Moses . . . using allegory had declared Paradise to be the womb . . . and Eden, the placenta . . ."

Here, within the Judeo-Christian patriarchal tradition, was an account of Creation that recalled the Mother, who is before all things, gave her spiritual and intellectual power, recognized Paradise as the female body. In this sense: Eden as mother-world.

When Marcus the Magician celebrates the mass, he teaches that wine is symbol of the Mother's blood. It is offered to the worshipper so that "Grace may flow" into those who drink it.

To partake of the mother in order to receive her power—that was the very repast the snake must have intended for Eve.

These were transitional texts, to be sure. They recalled the Mother but retained a tendency to ascribe her biological characteristics to the Father, so that one could see exactly how the original imagery had been torn from its female context in a reapportionment that was later to become so common in medieval Christian imagery. "The Word is everything to the child, both father and mother, teacher and nurse . . . the nutriment is the milk of the Father . . . and the Word alone supplies us children with the milk of love, and only those who suck at this breast are truly happy. For this reason, seeking is called sucking; to those infants who seek the Word, the father's loving breasts supply milk."

I was delighted with the confusion of this literary conceit, for it made a clear association between eating and visionary seeking, between the word and the breast, although milk and breast had been relocated on the father's body. Apparently, the Gnostic texts were themselves at the crossroads, passing from the world of the Mother into that of the Father, reapportioning her qualities and characteristics, so that the capacities of nurturance, love, and intelligence were bizarrely imagined as physical parts of the male body. Nevertheless, this was the very clue for which I had been looking. It supported my idea that Eve, when she began to eat the sacred fruit, was sucking up the maternal wisdom.

Other Gnostic writings gave clear expression to a female voice, who comprehends opposites and contradictions, in precisely the way I had imagined they were contained in the first, childhood experience of the mother.

> For I am the first and the last
> I am the honored one and the scorned one
> I am the whore and the holy one
> I am the wife and the virgin
> I am the mother and the daughter . . .
>
> I am the one who has been hated everywhere
>   and who has been loved everywhere . . .
>
> I am the knowledge of my inquiry
>   and the finding of those who seek after me . . .
>
> I am the bread and my mind within
> I am the knowledge of my name . . .

I found this imagery astonishing, since it brought together so many of the themes with which I had been working. Here was woman as food, clearly associated with knowledge. I felt as if I were taking bites from a forbidden apple. Finally, I had discovered a female voice of revelation. And the voice of Eve, who gives birth and proclaims:

> "I am the portion of my mother,
>   and I am the mother,
> I am the woman,
>   and I am the virgin."

I had come far since the days in Ireland when I drove back from the mountains. Then, I would not have dared to imagine the creation of woman in the image of a goddess. Certainly, I would never have wondered whether God was himself a lie. Yet now, when I began to search through the Gnostic texts for their interpretation of the male God, I found these banned gospels filling in blanks in the Old Testament Creation story, giving the key protagonists motivations that finally made sense out of the story.

In the *Hypostasis of the Archons,* a mythological Creation drama is described in which the illusory nature of male power is embodied in the blind ruler Samael, also named Sakla ("fool") and called Yaldaboath, "he who blasphemes against the divine."

This masculine ruler, who is blind, a fool, and a blasphemer, claims to have been the sole creator, in an act highly reminiscent of the claim made by the Old Testament God.

"Their chief is blind; [because of his] Power and his ignorance [and his] arrogance he said . . . : 'It is I who am God; there is none [apart from me].'"

But the Gnostic text knows better and reminds him that he is in error. He is not the only God. He is part of a whole, an entirety that he has forgotten. He is a jealous usurper of the mother-world.

> When he said this, he sinned against [the Entirety]. And this speech got up to Incorruptibility; then there was a voice that came forth from Incorruptibility, saying, "You are mistaken Samael"—which is, "god of the blind."

The story goes on. It tells about the way Incorruptibility looked down into the region of the Waters, which were her Image, so that she might bring the Entirety into union with the Light. But the Authorities of Darkness, the male powers, tried to "lay hold" of her Image but could not because it was a Spirit.

Translating this into a contemporary idiom, we understand: Incorruptibility is female. She sees her image in the waters. She attempts to unite two realms that have been divided. The Authorities of Darkness, disturbed by their undertaking, try to rape her.

I was excited to discover this mythic restatement of my own theme, to find that in this ancient tale a powerful Goddess was engaged in the essential work of bringing together the mother- and father-world. It made sense that even she, with all her visionary power, would find the task difficult. That now the creation of man must arise directly from this epic drama of the struggle for wholeness.

The Authorities of Darkness have been trying to trap this female spirit, to get their hands on her, to stop her work. To further their aim they have decided to make from earth the form of a man so that she would behold her male counterpart and they could seize hold of her through him. They made a man, called Adam. But he remained for a long time upon the ground. The Authorities blew upon him; they persisted like storm winds, but they were too weak to make him rise. He had soul but no spirit, the text says. Soul, but no spirit! Vividly, I recalled the years of aridity, when I sat in the garden behind my house, unable to make myself rise and begin work. Then, I could not have imagined that a goddess would look upon me with favor. Now, I was reading a banned, heretical text in which the female spirit, whose Image had shone forth from the waters, beholds a creature of earth who could not rise without her, and comes to dwell with him. Union with the female spirit—that, acording to the Gnostic tale, is how a living soul is created.

I read on. The story took a familiar turn, before it roved off in a surprising direction. Once Adam has arisen, the Rulers gather together all the animals of the earth and bring them to Adam so that he might name them. They take Adam and put him in the Garden, that he might cultivate it. They issue a command that he might eat of all the fruit trees in the garden save only one, the tree of recognizing good and evil. But here, once again, a radical element slips into the tale. These blind Rulers did not understand what they said to Adam because of their own ignorance. They spoke in such a way that Adam might in fact go ahead and eat of the fruit.

This story, in a similar vein, is told also by another Gnostic text, called *On the Origin of the World.* Some points that remain obscure in the first text become clarified in the second. Together, they comprehend an account of Creation that preserves a meaning and intention well hidden in the Old Testament narrative, which uses such similar material to such different ends.

The Rulers cause a deep sleep to fall upon Adam. Then they take from his side a living woman. We, naturally enough at this crucial moment in the story, expect God to make his stock entrance and breathe life into Adam. But here it is woman who does the work. She looks around, beholds the man lying on the ground, goes to him, and says: "Arise, Adam." Adam wakes up. And now, as if he were familiar with both versions of the tale, he immediately makes clear who is the supreme power in his world.

He says: "It is you who have given me life; you will be called 'Mother of the Living,'—For it is she who is my mother. It is she who is the Physician, and the Woman and She Who Has Given Birth."

So it is that Adam acknowledges and names Eve, his mother.

But the Authorities are still trying to ensnare the female Spirit. That is the purpose for which they have created man, a lump of earth that cannot rise without the spirit of woman. They see Adam speaking to his female counterpart. They become enamored of her. "Come," they say to each other, "let us sow our seed in her." They chase her; she laughs at them for their witlessness and their blindness. But in their clutches she becomes a tree, which they defile, says the text, "foully."

At this point in my reading I could not remain at my desk. Here, finally, was the imagery for which I had been looking for so many months. Here was the unmistakable, dramatic moment in which the Female Soul, the Mother, becomes transformed into a tree. It was just as I had imagined all along. That tree, which had caused all the trouble, tempting the woman with the forbidden knowledge of its forbidden fruit, had everything to do with a powerful Mother Goddess, Mother of the Living, She Who Had Given Birth.

V

The book lay open beneath my lamp. I was tired, ready for bed, but I wanted to live once again through that extraordinary narrative moment in which female Spirit becomes tree and is threatened with rape and plunder by a male Authority. I did not imagine that I would soon find cause for greater excitement. Picking up the story where I had left off, I now learned how the female spiritual element split herself in two. The spiritual element remained in the tree. The "shadowy reflection resembling herself" became a carnal woman. Adam's mate. Somehow the old Gnostic story had managed to record the very splitting of the primordial female into Original Goddess and Patriarchal Wife.

The loss of an original female wholeness. This event, which shapes the narrative action of the Gnostic story, aligns the heretical tale of Adam and Eve with psychological concerns. Unlike the account in the Old Testament, which thoroughly disguises the problem, the Gnostic account of Creation gives to the primordial splitting of the female a central place in the human story.

For now that the carnal woman has been separated from her original identity with female power, an instructor is needed to restore the condition of union. Readers of the Old Testament will not easily guess the form in which this instructor will now be presented. But we, who have begun to savor the Gnostic fruit, may be able to anticipate what comes next.

The scene is familiar. A tree stands in the garden, it bears fruit. The carnal woman and the man of earth are aware of the tree. They have been told that they may not eat from it. They are in ignorance. So far, we might as well be in the Old Testament tale. It is the moment for the snake's dramatic entrance.

But here the snake who comes to counsel disobedience is an enlightenment figure, an Instructor. It is not the snake in the grass, the vile serpent, the fallen Lucifer. This snake is a wisdom teacher, the form in which the female spiritual principle now presents herself. She urges Adam and the carnal woman to eat the fruit of the tree, she exposes the true nature of the usurping ruler. The snake says: "With death you shall not die; for it was out of jealousy that he said this to you. Rather your eyes shall open and you shall come to be like gods, recognizing evil and good."

And so they eat, as we expect them to. The woman eats of the tree and gives the fruit to her husband, as she does in our own Creation tale. And here, too, both recognize that they are naked. But now suddenly the meaning of nakedness takes on an entirely unexpected significance, at least for those of us who hear this story against the background of the biblical text. For in the Gnostic tale Adam and the carnal Eve discover that they are naked not only in the flesh, but with respect to the "Spiritual Element."

I was fascinated by this new understanding of nakedness. I read over the lines several times to make sure. But no, there could be no doubt, this curious text from the early centuries of Christianity understood nakedness as a state of ignorance. When these children of Paradise eat from the mother tree they realize that they are "naked with regard to knowledge." In other words: one bite of the Goddess fruit and they realize that the story they have been told by the patriarchal God, blind usurper, false authority, envious ravisher, is not the only possible tale. One bite of the mother fruit and they become aware that there is something very fishy about the idea of a Creator who is exclusively male.

Yes, I thought. Finally. A motive to eat and share food that had nothing to do with gluttony or the failure to resist temptation. At last I could say with textual authority: Eve gave the forbidden fruit to Adam because she wanted him to have the knowledge she has come to possess by eating at the Mother Tree. Here at last, Eve's imperative disobedience.

I imagine the scene. I reinvent it. The anguish of the woman who has eaten. Who knows that her husband is still blind. There she is, with a single bite of the apple, light years ahead of him. She knows that the male Authority in the garden has puffed himself up with a false grandiosity, has been lording it over them out of ignorance.

What will she do? Pretend she knows nothing? It's all still the same? Nothing has happened? Yet she is aware of a strange power; she has dared to eat truth. She has consumed the Mother Goddess. With this act she has left Adam behind in his naïve dream of filial obedience, loyal to a false God who pretends to be the Creator. She is overcome by loneliness. Where is he? This man whom she had called husband, imagined equal? She must find him and make him eat.

But what about the expulsion from the garden? Would the Gnostic texts rework the Old Testament reading of the Creation story on this point, too? I turned the pages of the book, dazzled by the possibility. Eve, the sinner, had already been restored to her primal connection with the

Mother Goddess. But then, why expell her from the garden for eating the fruit that had given her back this knowledge?

In *The Hypostasis of the Archons* the motive is clear: the expulsion has been arranged by those false masculine authorities that had wished all along to keep Eve and Adam ignorant of their origins. The "Authorities" cast Eve and Adam from the garden and cursed them and drove them into a life of toil so that they "might be occupied by worldly affairs, and might not have the opportunity of being devoted to the Holy Spirit," mother of everything. Here was the expulsion, not as punishment for disobedience, but as an act of jealous revenge.

This detail, so wondrously mysterious in its own right, began to take on further significance as I placed it in context. Here was Eve, expelled from the father's house, kicked out of the garden, driven into a life of toil, damned to perpetual busy-ness so that she would not have time to worship the Holy One. However, as a direct consequence of this expulsion, she is left with the responsibility for creating the human race. A strange punishment, is it not? Scarcely a curse, certainly nothing to lament for thousands of years, no matter who is telling the story. And now it seemed to me that embedded even in the biblical narrative there was a coded message, one that the biblical editors had not been able to suppress. The expulsion, intended in one story to punish Eve, in another to separate her from the Holy Spirit, in both succeeds in doing just the reverse. By expelling Eve, the arrogant male Authority (read either text) restores to Eve her original power as creator of life, thereby reestablishing her hidden identity with the Great Mother. Read like this, the expulsion allows Eve's return to her true nature; the Fall brings about her rise to creative power.

I was beginning to have a deep respect for storytelling, and for the way ancient images and figures continue to tell their own story, no matter how hard someone is trying to deflect their meaning. The tree, the snake, the apple, the woman eating, the wrath of a jealous God, the expulsion from the garden. No matter how much they were transposed, rewoven, and reworked, all ended in the same place, with Eve as the mother of the human race. But there really was no other possibility. This is, after all, a story about the way the human race was created. Even the most perverse storyteller knows that a male God cannot give birth. Sooner or later he's going to have to have a woman do the work for him.

But why hadn't I read the Creation drama like this before, as a testament to female creativity? Why had it taken the Gnostic Gospels, these banned and buried documents, to make me aware of the hidden meaning of the story? Evidently there was something about the way the tale was told in the Old Testament that assured Eve's creative power would not easily be recognized. Perhaps, even, it was the revelation of this distinctively female power that had caused the Gnostic texts to be suppressed?

The biblical story was told on behalf of a jealous God—jealous of Eve's power to create life. And so, in the Old Testament story, woman's ability to give birth is transposed into a biological curse, a toil, a limitation, instead of being celebrated as a creative force analogous to the power of a Goddess.

Nevertheless, the jealous storytellers were not quite able to pull it off. There is a shadow of inevitable fate and self-contradiction hovering over the Old Testament tale. An all-knowing God, who therefore foresees the consequence of planting the tree of knowledge in his garden and yet plants it there, it is said, to exercise man in the freedom of will with which God has endowed him. But it is also said that woman does not have those virtues that make freedom of choice possible. God, who made her like that, must have known she was stubborn, disobedient, headstrong, gluttonous. He must have known that if the tree of (female) knowledge was in the garden she'd go after it, break the taboo, eat, and be cursed.

Why would he, the loving Father, create this inexorable drama unless he had no choice? But that is precisely the point. God the Father had none. The tree appeared in the garden because it was the Mother Tree, the missing female half of this posturing, false creator.

The Lord God, and those who told his story, were unable to evade this basic knowledge that birth is a female act. They might curse it, pretend to despise it, make it seem the painful outcome of a sinful deed, but fundamentally they could not do without it.

The Eden story could not unfold from the creation of man in the image of a male god. It would have been stuck there, with the man able to do only what the god was able to do—endlessly, narcissistically, impotently, shape from dust a male capable of shaping another man of dust.

If the human race is to be created, a woman will have to do it. The male God will need to create a disobedient woman. If then he still cannot deal with his envy; if it isn't enough to have turned the all-powerful Mother into a sinful daughter, the whole encumbering arsenal of taboo and curse and punishment will have to be grafted on to the Creation story, which, nevertheless, as stories do, comes out in the end where it started in the first place. Woman as Creator. It is inevitable.

At this point in the drama the Gnostic Gospels had added a very dear and characteristic note. Until now, I was reading old tales in which familiar characters were dressed up in new symbolic clothes. But now suddenly, as I turned the pages of my book, I came across a person who adapted herself to my storytelling purposes far more completely than I could have dared hope. For Eve, after she begot Cain and Abel and Seth, suddenly became pregnant again. What's this? I thought. Eve pregnant a fourth time? Who knows what she might now bring forth? I held my breath. Could it be? And Eve said: "He has begotten on [me a] virgin as an assistance [for] many generations of mankind."

Yes, Eve gave birth to a daughter. Eve gave birth to a virgin who had never been defiled by the "Forces" in the father garden. Eve gave birth to a girl named Norea to help in the creation of humankind.

In this respect, too, the Gnostic Gospels were kinder to Eve than was the Old Testament. And who knows? Maybe a woman was telling the Gnostic story in the first place? Maybe a woman who had given birth? "What?" she says to herself, I imagine. "One woman with the task of creating the whole human race? Poor Eve. I better give her a daughter."

I had a feeling, the moment I heard of Norea, that I was going to like her. She, who was born to help her mother create humanity—what kind of woman, I wondered, was this Norea? Born after the expulsion, she had never known the Father's garden, where the Rulers and Authorities had tried so hard to usurp the Mother's power. She came to life outside that arrogant garden of a punitive god, where the mother-root is denied and the female spirit raped and plundered. She, I thought, would have been a proud, free spirit, afraid of nothing. She knows that she has been birthed for the purpose of creating the generations that will come after her. Was this she at last? Daughter of the New Eve? The Woman Who Is Not Yet?

In the Gnostic texts, the Rulers come to meet Norea.

They hope to lead her astray. They are still trying to capture female power. They come to Norea and they lie to her. "Your mother Eve came to us," they say, suggesting that Eve was a harlot. But Norea doesn't bite. She says: "It is you who are the Rulers of Darkness; you are accursed. And you did not know my mother . . . I am not your descendant; rather it is from the World Above that I am come."

The Authorities try again. They have created this entire drama as a lure for the female spirit. If rape is insufficient to damage the mother's reputation, the Authority will lie; it will tarnish the very name of woman. In the Gnostic tale, the arrogant Ruler turns with all his might. His countenance darkens. He says to Norea: "You must render service to us [as did] your mother Eve . . ."

But he is dealing with the Woman Who Is Not Yet. She will not let herself be tricked into believing Eve is a whore, a great sinner. How shall we read this detail? Could it mean that Norea refuses to regard the act of sexual congress, which leads to birth, as a degraded activity? That she refuses to conceive the female capacity to give birth as an inferior form of creativity? Norea knows exactly what to do. She will not let herself be raped or intimidated. She turns and cries out in a loud voice, calling upon the Holy One to save her from the "Rulers of Unrighteousness." To save her, she says, "from their clutches." She calls upon the Holy One to prevent the rape of Eve's daughter.

An angel descends and takes her to task. He wants to know why she acts so boldly toward the Holy Spirit. It is an angel of awesome power, with an appearance of fine gold and raiment of snow. It is called the Great Angel, of terrifying sublimity. But Eve's daughter is not afraid. Boldly she speaks up. "Who are you?" she demands to know.

The angel, responsive to her daring, reveals its identity. "It is I who am Eleleth, Sagacity, the Great Angel who stands in the presence of the Holy Spirit . . . I shall teach you about your Root."

So it is that Eve's daughter receives instruction. In a scene entirely reminiscent of the patriarchal tale told by Milton, in which Adam receives instruction from the Archangel Gabriel, Norea now learns the true nature of things. This is what I imagine Norea learned: female creative power has its roots in biological creativity. Woman is not less than man because she gives birth. She is, simply, the Creator.

The Angel, Understanding, talks to Norea about the "limitless realms" of Incorruptibility, of Sophia, called Pistis. Norea learns that Sophia Pistis wanted to "create something alone without her consort" and that "her product was a celestial thing." And now Eleleth tells the story of Creation all over again. A veil stretched between the World Above and the realms below. A shadow shaped beneath the veil. It was an aborted creature, part of matter. It was a being, arrogant as a beast, resembling a lion. It was androgynous but referred to as "he."

"Opening his eyes he saw a vast quantity of Matter without limit; and he became arrogant, saying, 'It is I who am God, and there is none other apart from me.'"

This, according to the Gnostic tale, is the true story of Creation as revealed to Eve's daughter Norea. It is a tale about the creation of an arrogant God who denies his origins in the Mother. A blind God, who imagines that his world of dead matter is all that matters. A God who creates a vast realm for himself to rule over. A God who has split himself off from the light of the Mother—and who therefore, let us note, must inevitably become jealous of the female creative power he can never find in himself. That (in so many words) is the Understanding imparted to the daughter of the woman who ate the wisdom-apple, who was cast out of the garden of ignorance, to create a daughter who speaks to angels, who tell the truth about the Mother Tree.

That is the tale of Norea, in whose name the woman we are shaping must now be fashioned.

VI

The lump of mud I had propped up on my desk, between the collected works of Freud and my reader's edition of the Bible, was still changing. I was not aware of having taken it in hand since I began brooding over the Gnostic texts. Yet I wasn't at all surprised to discover that this mud-pie woman had acquired genitals. She was still young. There was no hair under her arms or between her legs. But she was a comely maiden, I thought, her sex ripening and flowering in its wisdom.

The face of my little woman was still featureless, inexpressive. But that, I told myself, was to be expected. I was not yet through with the work of transformation that was to redeem Eve and her appetite. I picked up the clay. It seemed to me that something had changed above the neck. I held it up to the light and looked at it closely. Yes, on the left side of the head, the clay was shaping a circular object that now began to take the rough, expressive form of an ear.

I laughed. This little creature, who did not yet have a mouth, seemed to be talking. It's all well and good, she was saying, in a muffled voice that had a distinctly Old World inflection. You can make what you like out of these old stories. But don't forget. It is you who brought me back out of the underworld. And therefore I belong not merely to the ancient Hebrews and their neighbors and not only to that tribe of Goddess-worshippers whose story you are telling in your novel. This clay you have dredged up out of your own primordial ooze must be made in your image, too. You are a woman who has been trying to weave an understanding of female development. You can't just take up the old symbols and restore them to their old meanings. You, if you recall, are not only a storyteller.

I wanted to argue with her. Psychologists, I thought to say, are storytellers, too. They like to present their tales as a science and to describe their speculations as theories. But we don't have to be taken in by this. Freud said what we had to say by talking about Oedipus. Jung borrowed freely and gratefully from the heroes and monsters of old tales. Psychology, I thought to insist, is a disguised form of storytelling, exploiting the story's inexhaustible ability to yield new meaning.

But I was wondering where her voice came from. Was it possible the future woman will speak from an ear on the left side of her head? Then I remembered. It was up to me to complete this figure. I looked at its mud face. Had I been hesitating to give it a mouth? A mouth that spoke clearly and received food?

Eve had come back with me out of the fertile darkness of the underworld to be inscribed with my understanding of female hunger. Her appetite in the patriarchal garden has everything in common with our hunger for a future as women. Hidden within our longing for food there is a Goddess hunger—forbidden to us, as it was also to Eve, when she emerged from Adam's side in the biblical Eden.

Apples, figs, pomegranates, peaches, milk shakes, Mother's Cookies—they are emblems of the Great Mother who fed us at her ripe breasts during our first sojourn in Paradise. That is why eating seems forbidden and food dangerous. When we eat we know. That is what the old stories tell us. What we know from eating will always lead back through a wandering train of primordial association to the mother-ground of first experience, before the father stole the garden, usurped the mother's power, established himself in her place.

When the biblical scribes borrowed Eve from the Mideastern stories about her, they lifted her from the mother's house and set her down in a patriarchal realm. In doing so, they unwittingly took her through the developmental sequence a woman in our culture also knows when she comes to the crossroads and leaves the mother-world behind, forgetting it and the goddess who established it.

The Old Eve has an uncanny similarity to the diminished women we have become. In the patriarchal garden Eve is not Hawweh, who creates the human race, a carnal woman recently separated from the primordial Mother Tree. Here, she has forgotten all about the primordial woman who gave her life. Therefore she has also forgotten she was once a Goddess.

Eve, in the father's garden, is told that a male God created her in his image. We have been told the same tall story. She, too, has to make sense of herself as a female shaped from a disposable part of male anatomy. He, the loyal son of patriarchy, is obedient, he is not tempted by hunger, he is in perfect command of his bodily desires. She, the afterthought, is gluttonous, succumbs easily to temptation, surrenders without much struggle to her body's wish to eat. When hunger wakes her she regards it as a snake, dangerous, forbidden, diabolical. Eve imagines her hunger a temptation she should resist.

The hunger-snake has a good piece of work to face. The snake must get Eve to see that the future of woman demands her disobedience. Whatever we are not supposed to know or do, Eve must find out and accomplish. Whatever we are forbidden must be allowed to us. Somehow Eve must come to understand that by inhabiting her body and its desires she will be restored to her full potential as her mother's daughter.

They say: she violated the taboo, surrendered to the snake, ate the apple, corrupted the man, brought about the expulsion from the Father's garden, was responsible for the Fall, called down the Father's curse. Upon earth, upon labor, upon childbirth, upon woman. So far as they were concerned they told a tale of sin and its punishment, of gluttony and its consequences, of disobedience and the revenge taken by the primal father against those who eat.

I say: Eve dared to break the taboo against eating, embraced the temptation offered by the snake, ate the apple, and returned symbolically to the maternal breast to regain an identity with the Mother Goddess. If eating caused her to be expelled from her Father's house, that precisely is what allowed her to give birth to the Woman Who Is Not Yet.

Eve's dilemma: a choice between obedience and knowledge. Between renunciation and appetite. Between subordination and desire. Between security and risk. Between loyalty and self-development. Between submission and power. Between hunger as temptation and hunger as vision.

It is the dilemma of modern women.

The New Eve began to look at me with excitement. She was flexing her muscles, kicking out her legs, running a few steps, leaping into the air. I saw her eying the walls that still closed her in the father-world, where Adam was packing his bags and hurrying to keep her company as she set off. He was man, shaped to loyalty and not to rebellion, but he had cast his lot with her. His hunger had been met by Eve and her mother-fruit.

"Listen," I said. I was worried about Eve's restlessness. "It's not time yet for the great leap forward. Believe me, I know all about your impatience. I too have been standing in front of the tree for years. But now, before you leap out of the Father's garden, why not hesitate one moment longer, see what it might be like to go after that apple in full knowledge of what it means to eat it?"

We walked together, the new Eve and I, making our way to the Mother Tree. I looked closely at her: guide, exemplar, foremother, counselor, ancestress. Made from our clay, she would soon give birth, would inscribe the female sex with courage, visionary zeal, the capacity for taking risk, an irresistible hunger for knowledge. She was on the way to her epic act of disobedience.

It was a warm, still day of the kind you find often in Eden. Clear skies of a soft blue hung by the Mother with loving care. I noticed a flowering shrub. Milk oozed from it. A lullaby blew its breath on us. The moon hung in the west, cradled by a sun that had not yet risen. Darkness and light held the garden in equal measure. Owls cooed, doves hooted, a chariot of winged angels sailed by overhead. Fires burned along the path that led to the Mother Tree, where a stork stood in the pool from which Eve had once awakened under a shade of flowers, in her mother's lap.

The snake came out to join us. She had been watching our progress from the woods but now she came with an open mouth and one hand outstretched, pointing to the Tree of Life. I thought she was a beautiful creature, but Eve drew back, clutching my arm with dread.

"Do it, do it," I urged, from a child's sense of delight in what should not be done. The garden was still. Black sheep grazed quietly; from the distance I heard the rattle of leaves. Light was flooding down from a sky withdrawing behind veils of blue light. The stones were speaking.

Eve stood a long time in front of the tree. It had happened so many times, in so many stories, and each time there had been the same terror and hesitation. Maybe the Rulers and the Authorities and blind Samael and the Father God were telling the truth? Maybe death awaited her? The snake stood watching. She had pointed the way to the tree. All voices were silent. It was up to Eve.

Then finally, moving in the bold grace of a woman who has grown back into her body, with a gesture that had freed itself from all dread of hunger, Eve reached out and touched the fruit. The tree split itself in two. A woman stepped from it, holding her breasts with both hands. And now, as she came toward us, the snake went to nest in her hair. In the grove next to the pool the lion lay down with the lamb. The angel Eleleth parked her chariot at the crossroads and the tree grew whole. It put forth apples and figs and peaches and pomegranates, while doves and oysters and cherubs and pigs came to nestle in its branches, to cast down upon us her freely given, never forbidden, freshly primordial fruit.

Notes

Page xvii   Maxine Mrantz, *Women of Old Hawaii*, Honolulu: Aloha Graphics, 1975.

Page xviii   Interesting discussions of this relationship between Goddess and apple can be found in Joseph Campbell, *The Mythic Image*, Princeton: Princeton University Press, 1974; Robert Graves, *The White Goddess*, New York: Vintage Books, 1958; Erich Neumann, *The Great Mother: An Analysis of the Archetype*, Princeton: Princeton University Press, 1963; Barbara Walker, *The Woman's Encyclopedia of Myths and Secrets*, New York: Harper & Row, 1983.

Page xx   Carl Olsen, *The Book of the Goddess*. New York: Crossroad, 1983.

Page 9   Alice Koller, *An Unknown Woman: A Journey to Self-Discovery*, New York: Bantam, 1981.

Page 13   I have since found a discussion of the pig as sacred animal of the Vegetation Goddess in Marija Gimbutas, *The Goddesses and Gods of Old Europe*, Berkeley: University of California Press, 1982.

Page 19   *An Interrupted Life: The Diaries of Etty Hillesum 1941–1943*, New York: Pantheon Books, 1983.

Page 24   Elaine Pagels, *The Gnostic Gospels*, New York: Random House, 1979.

Page 28   A fascinating discussion of the archaeological discoveries of Goddess figures and figurines can be found in Wolfgang Lederer, *The Fear of Women*, New York: Grune and Stratton, 1968.

Page 28   A brilliant discussion of Old Europe, and the dominance of women in society, can be found in Gimbutas, op. cit.

Page 30   The mother holding her massive breasts is described by Patricia Monaghan, *The Book of Goddesses and Heroines*, New York: E.P. Dutton, 1981. This book is a superb source for information about goddesses and heroines from many cultures.

Page 32   The poem spoken on behalf of the female divine presence can be found in James M. Robinson, ed., *The Nag Hammadi Library in English*, San Francisco: Harper & Row, 1977.

Page 32   The story of Eve giving life to Adam can be found in Robinson, ed., op. cit.

Page 51   Friedrich Nietzsche, *The Birth of Tragedy*, New York: Doubleday Anchor Books, 1956.

Page 62   Quotations from women's diaries will be found in Mary Jane Moffat and Charlotte Painter, eds., *Revelations: Diaries of Women*, New York: Vintage Books, 1974.

Page 67   Harry Guntrip, *Psychoanalytic Theory, Therapy, and the Self*, New York: Basic Books, 1971.

Page 82   My source for these references to the underworld is the extremely important and arresting book, Walker, *The Women's Encyclopedia of Myths and Secrets*, op. cit.

Page 87   All quotations from Freud in the following pages are from Sigmund Freud, *Civilization and Its Discontents*, New York: W. W. Norton & Co., 1961.

Page 89   The discussion of regression is from Calvin Hall, *A Primer of Freudian Psychology*, New York: Mentor Books, 1979.

Page 97   Catherine Luquet-Parat's article, "The Change of Object," can be found in Janine Chasseguet-Smirgel, *Female Sexuality: New Psychoanalytic Views*, Ann Arbor: University of Michigan Press, 1970.

Page 98   Nancy Chodorow, *The Reproduction of Mothering: Psychoanalysis and the Sociology of Gender*, Berkeley: University of California Press, 1978.

Page 98   A fascinating discussion of female sexuality can also be found in Jeanne Lampl-De Groot, "The Evolution of the

Oedipus Complex in Women," 1927, in Robert Fliess, ed., *The Psychoanalytic Reader: An Anthology of Essential Papers with Critical Introductions*, New York: International Universities Press, 1969.

Page 103   "The poet" is Gerard Manley Hopkins. The poem is "God's Grandeur," in W. H. Gardner, ed., *Gerard Manley Hopkins: A Selection of His Poems and Prose*, Middlesex: Penguin Books, 1953.

Page 137   A discussion of "berches" will be found in Hayyim Schauss, *The Jewish Festivals: History and Observance*, New York: Schocken Books, 1962.

Page 142   "The Uncertainty of Eve" can be found in Kim Chernin, *The Hunger Song*, London: Menard Press, 1983.

Page 149   John Milton, "Paradise Lost," in Merritt Y. Hughes, ed., *John Milton: Complete Poems and Major Prose*, New York: The Odyssey Press, 1957.

Pages 149–51   The various folk sayings and quotations in the following pages can be found in Leo Rosten, *Treasury of Jewish Quotations*, New York: McGraw Hill, 1972; Frank S. Mead, ed., *The Encyclopedia of Religious Quotations*, Westwood, N.J.: Fleming H. Revell Co., 1965; H. L. Mencken, ed., *A New Dictionary of Quotations on Historical Principles from Ancient and Modern Sources*, New York: Alfred A. Knopf, 1942.

Page 155   The story of Eve creating a phallus is in Robert Graves, *The Greek Myths*, New York: Penguin Books, 1955.

Page 155   A fascinating discussion of Eve, the serpent and the Goddess can be found in Merlin Stone, *When God Was a Woman*, New York: Harcourt Brace Jovanovich, 1976.

Page 155   The story of Eurynome is in Robert Graves and Raphael Patai, *Hebrew Myths*, New York: Doubleday & Co., 1964.

Page 155   The story about the Female Spiritual Principle is *The Hypostasis of the Archons*, Robinson, ed., op. cit.

Page 156   Great Mother Hsi Wang Mu and her magic peaches is described in Walker, op. cit.

Page 156   The Goddess Hathor is discussed in Stone, op. cit.

Page 156   The Great Goddess as a vegetative symbol and feeder of the dead is discussed in Neumann, op. cit.

Although I do not quote from it directly, the most comprehensive, authoritative, and beautiful book written on the Great Goddess is undoubtedly Theodor H. Gaster, ed., Sir James George Frazer, *The New Golden Bough*, New York: Anchor Books, 1961.

Page 156   Xikum, the divine fig tree, is described in Walker, op. cit.

Page 161   I came home from the bookstore with four books, all of them likely to be of interest to anyone interested in Gnostic literature. They are: Hans Jonas, *The Gnostic Religion: The Message of the Alien God and the Beginnings of Christianity*, Boston: Beacon Press, 1958; G. R. S. Mead, *Pistis Sophia: A Gnostic Miscellany*, London: John M. Watkins, 1963; Pagels, op. cit.; Robinson, ed., op. cit.

Page 162   Quotations from the Gnostic Gospels here and in the following pages can be found in Pagels, op. cit., and in Robinson, ed., op. cit. The interpretations of the texts are, of course, my own.

Acknowledgments

Michael Rogin, Elisabeth Scharlatt, Diane Cleaver, Elizabeth Abel, and Roz Parenti have read this manuscript, discussed it with me, and talked with me about and inspired many of the ideas in this work. Renate Stendhal, in addition, edited the manuscript. I am delighted to thank all of them for their help, humor, cunning, and friendship.

Permissions Acknowledgments

About the Author

Kim Chernin is the author of three previous nonfiction works, *The Hungry Self, In My Mother's House,* and *The Obsession.* She has written a novel, *The Flame Bearers,* and a book of poetry, *The Hunger Song.* Ms. Chernin lives in Berkeley, California, where she is in private practice.